Seasons of the Leelanau

Sandra Serra Bradshaw

Northmont Publishing, Inc.
West Bloomfield, Michigan

We gratefully acknowledge Traverse Tall Ship Company, Schooners *Malibu* and *Manitou,* Sugar Loaf Resort, and National Parks Service-Sleeping Bear Dunes National Lakeshore for contributing the cover photos.

Northmont Publishing, Inc.
6346 Orchard Lake Road, #201
West Bloomfield, Michigan 48322

© 1994 by Sandra Serra Bradshaw.   All rights reserved

Printed in the United States of America

96   95   94   93   5   4   3   2   1

ISBN 1-878005-71-5

Illustrations by Mary Bain

Map by Suzan Moody

Designed by Mary Primeau

Edited by Thomas B. Seller

To my sons,
Forrest
and Cameron

Contents

Foreword
Introduction
1. The Essence of Leelanau
2. A Town-by-Town Guide in History
3. The Native Americans
4. Leelanau Lodging
5. Dining, Leelanau-Style
6. Gift Shops and Galleries
7. Fruit of the Leelanau
8. Seasons of the Maritime
9. The Sleeping Bear Dunes National Lakeshore
10. Fishing and Boating the Seasons of the Leelanau
11. Seasons of Recreation
12. Seasonal Reflections and Promises

Appendix
    DNR Access Sites
    National and State Registers of Historic Sites
    References

Foreward

All 16,500-plus of us who live here know how special Leelanau County is. As an occasional writer about my county, I hear many of our visitors tell us how special they find it to be. Gov. William G. Milliken spoke of its "splendor." Gov. James J. Blanchard called it "Paradise." Gov. John Engler said its Sleeping Bear Dunes form part of a tapestry that makes "Michigan's shoreline the most beautiful in all the states."

Leelanau was named in 1840 by ethnologist Henry Rowe Schoolcraft, a federal Indian agent whose extensive writings on the history and conditions of native Americans were an important inspirational source of legends for Henry Wadsworth Longfellow's lyric epic, The *Song of Hiawatha*. Schoolcraft said Leelinau, as it was originally spelled, meant "delight of life," as he chronicled in the *Legend of Leelinau* about an Indian maiden attracted to her sylvan land of delight. From this comes the county's modern-day slogan: "Land of Delight."

This land of delight is also a land of creativity. Artists abound in Leelanau. So do authors. Sandra Serra Bradshaw, creator of this book, is one of the newest. She provides a delightful mix of fact and fancy—a poetic guide book through the seasons, sights, and shops of Leelanau.

Just as the shimmering whiteness of Leelanau's Sleeping Bear Dunes was a beacon to those who first traveled by water, it was a landmark for the first space travelers. U.S. astronaut Jack Lousma, who climbed the dunes as a boy growing up in Michigan and viewed them from 200 and 275 miles away in two space missions, told me: "Sleeping Bear really stands out from space."

From ground zero, the whole county stands out. Sandy Bradshaw helps us find our way.

      —George Weeks
      Columnist, *The Detroit News*
      Author, *Sleeping Bear: Its Lore, Legends, and First People* and
      Sleeping Bear: Yesterday and Today

Acknowledgements

Many people were involved in the accomplishment of Seasons of the Leelanau, at both the infancy of the book down to its final editing, production, and distribution. Here are a few that were especially involved, in one way or another. If I have overlooked someone, it is unintentional.

Nick Altwerger and Bob Mandel of A&M Publishing. The editor, Tom Seller, who patiently guided me along. Ken Scott and his book *Michigan's Leelanau County*, who introduced me to A&M Publishing. Lauren Collins, who introduced me to Ken and Suzan Moody at The Lazy Lodge, where much of this book was created amid the deer, the pine, and the waters, which provided added inspiration, and where Suzan's assistance became indispensable. Dr. Steven Johnson, for encouragement when I needed it most. George and Mollie Weeks, for their invaluable advice and encouragement; George wrote the foreword and introductory material on Glen Arbor shops. Suzanne Latta, for helpful library references. Laura Quackenbush, curator of the Leelanau Museum, for historical background and guidance along with Ruth Atkinson. Mallie Marshall and Prudence Mead, for their vote of confidence. Beverly Gilmore, Grace Dickinson Johnson, and Fred and Julia Dickinson, for special encouragement and support; Julia wrote the sketches of Glen Arbor and Empire in chapter 2. Ranger Bill Herd of the Sleeping Bear Dunes National Lakeshore, for his tremendous input and information on the park. Bill Skolnic, Mary Blue, and Larry Mawby, who taught me a bit about wine making; Bill wrote the section "From Grapes to Wine" in chapter 7. John Elder, for information on the tall ships. Jon Smith, and especially Gerald Castino, for much needed guidance on the fishing section. Bill Carlson, for historical information on Fishtown. Doug McCormick for sharing his years of nautical wisdom. Bill Klintworth, for his professional assistance. Kevin Herman, for his review of the cherry industry. Eric Currin at Computer Doctor, Jim and Mike Pendergast at Bitsystems, and Jim Moss, for technical computer assistance. Owen Bahle and Helen Wransky, for historical assistance; Helen wote the part on Suttons Bay history. John P. Kilcherman, for his enthusiastic information on historical apples. Pete Edwards, for his upbeat attitude, encouragement, and information about Sugar Loaf Resort. Ann Marie Mitchell, for kindly and extensive information on the Homestead Resort. Cher Andrade, for her description of the Leelanau Scenic Railroad. Fred and Betty Sincock, Dave Taghon, Tom Meister, Sarah Mead, Penny Mace, Dianna Oberschulte, Mona Kay Beldin, and Scott Jones for contributing information. Orlun Jones, for his encouragement and understanding from southern California, while the book was under way. Gordon and Marilyn Sellars, Dick and Em Sprankle, Mike and Laura O'Connor, Pat Cookman, Greg and Leanne Wares, John and Theresa Fochtman, Monica Weaver, Jim Hawley, Richard Plamondon, Judy Hayes-Daly, and Chrissy Parham for their special support. With deepest appreciation to Gerald and Jacqueline Scott at Flying Scott Farm. Naomi Kline, for telling me to "go find my dream up north." Dr. Dennis Stanford, for the "trilliums in the sandy earth." To "The Leelanau Twelve," a very special thank-you. And to my father, Anthony, with love.

Introduction

As a gift and publisher's trade representative of Northern Networks, a company I formed after moving to the Leelanau, I saw a need for a book such as this one. First of all, being a newcomer I realized I didn't know much about this beautiful place I now called home. Leaving my little lakefront home down state and moving up north proved to be challenging and even scary at times. It was like packing a suitcase and going on a vacation, never to return.

I approached each day during the first years as if opening a gift exquisitely wrapped. Yes, there is much to discover and experience in Leelanau. Ancient and more recent history come to life as one tours the area. There are legends to explore, artists to discover, countless lovely shops and galleries. The beaches and the lakes are among the world's most beautiful. No one can get bored during a stay here; it's just too beautiful a place.

And the people! For the most part they are such a joy, so full of energy and talent. I came up with a formula to describe our residents; it's called "the three R's." To live here, one must either be rich, retired, or resourceful. You will be meeting some of these unique people in chapter twelve.

The purpose of this book is to acquaint the newcomer with the area

Introduction

and to allow residents to discover more of what Leelanau has to offer, in both a historical and present-day context. Though the contents of this book took over a year and a half of research and writing, believe me there is lots more out there to discover. This project easily could have taken up several years devoted to research and discovery. I hope I've covered the best of Leelanau; if I've overlooked something please let me know.

   I came to realize that while writing this book, along with my great love for this beautiful piece of God's country, I could offer both the enthusiasm of a newcomer and the seasonings of a representative and business owner who has to keep up with the beat of what is happening.

   I sincerely hope that you find the book accurate, informative, and, most of all, interesting.

The Essence of Leelanau

Leelanau! Leelanau! "Land of Delight"!
Majestic are her hills, her land.
Surrounded by water, sunrise, sunset
Touching her shores of sand.

When one first enters this Leelanau, this "Land of Delight," no matter what the season the usual first impression is awe. As time and distance encompass one, the appreciation builds to a near reverence of this lovely spot, the "little finger" of Michigan's mitten-shaped Lower Peninsula. Michigan's motto is especially true of the Leelanau peninsula: "If you seek a lovely peninsula just look around you."

The waters on her lakes are many various shades of blues and greens, sometimes gentle and quiet and at other times windswept and awesome in their power.

The land is sculpted with many hills, some so steep that the skies look like mountains behind them. Others are more rolling, many planted with cherries—oh, the cherries, so lovingly cultivated for so

The Essence of Leelanau

many generations and seasons past and seasons to come. There are the Leelanau's massive dune areas, windswept and also changing with each season. These are a sacred ground, something to be deeply respected for the fragility of this land and for the power the dunes evoke.

The sunrises and sunsets that claim Leelanau are a beautiful rite of their own. On the peninsula one gets the delight of wakening to a sunrise and the pleasure of a sunset over water.

Sunrise touches Grand Traverse Bay before the hills are gently wakened. One notices a lightening in the east, which gradually turns into a pinkish hue, and then—sunrise. A vast ball of crimson begins to blaze over the waters and land, the beginning of a new day.

Sunsets can be described only as majestic and thought provoking as one watches this fiery ball slip deeper and deeper into Lake Michigan's horizon. As one travels through the gentle hills and valleys at sunset, one is bathed in an immense golden glow, which slowly gives way to evening's quiet darkness.

Each season of the Leelanau is fresh, offering both the visitor and resident something new to discover, experience, or explore. From the start of early spring, snow still amassed on her beaches and hills, there is memorable spring skiing, for both the cross-country and downhill skiers. Getting off the beaten track, although none is so civilized as to be overused, you can find private vistas over her bays and the Great Lake, where it takes your breath away.

Maple trees are in abundance in this area, producing the sweet sap to turn into maple syrup. Wildflowers, too, are found everywhere. In spring there are masses of trilliums in the wooded areas. At first their lovely white petals are tinged with green in their veins. Later some turn a salmon pink. They are definitely worth a stop to admire. But please do not pick; they are on the ever-growing list of protected species. In the wetter areas of the county, bogs are filled with swamp marigolds on display in their brilliant yellow. Morels, too, can be found here; the county some years has an abundance of this delectable mushroom.

The cherry trees, acres and acres of them, begin their show sometime in late spring depending on the weather. Their blossoms look like balls of snowflakes perched on their branches. The sight and fragrance of the cherry blossoms in bloom is unforgettable as fresh spring air mixes with the clean westerly breezes off Lake Michigan. Soon one finds the trees loaded down with little red cherries, a sharp contrast to the pointed green leaves and the heavenly blue skies above. They make up handsomely for the lost sight of the blossoms. Soon the tastes of tarts and sweets will tempt the palate, and roadside stands everywhere will beckon the passerby with signs that read Cherries, Cherries.

Early June is a quiet time as the beaches lie silent awaiting the first bare feet to dare the waters. The local tall ships have been sailing for some time now, filled with eager students and visitors savoring the cool waters and breezes while aboard. On shore the distant admirer watches the tall ships as they silently and ever so majesti-

cally glide over the waters, while smaller fishing boats dot the poetic scene. The towns across the peninsula are still waking from the winter past. Many stores are just opening, and those that have been open all winter are eager for the summer visitors and festivals soon to advance upon them. But the quiet time now is also something to enjoy, for it will not be experienced again until nearly hunting season. As summer arrives the tempo and the warmth of the waters rise steadily, together welcoming the visitors, who come from everywhere and gently fill this quiet, clean land. The migrant workers and their families have arrived, mostly from Texas and Florida, a part of the cherry industry for so many seasons past and seasons to come.

Early September brings a softness and a quietness to the Leelanau. Even the air seems to change to an often smoky haze over her hills, waters, and lakes, this even before fall's majestic dance of colors begin their parade. It is a wonderful time to come and explore; the beaches lie quiet, still yearning for company, solitary walks provide an escape rare in these times. Shopkeepers are now taking a breather, but still anxious for the visitors before the long winter sets in with her seal. It is a great time to shop; lots of bargains make way for a new season, a new year.

And then October. What a sight to behold in the Leelanau! Michigan, so well known for her color spectacular in autumn, has given the peninsula a great share in this display. Hike the National Lakeshore by woods or field. Drive past the apple orchards dripping heavily with several kinds of apple species. See the rolling hills draped with such beautiful extravaganza. See the azure blues of her bays, lakes, and the power of Lake Michigan. Often you will glimpse freighters camped in Suttons Bay, taking refuge from November's rath and Lake Michigan's changing fury. Canoe the Crystal River, admire her gentleness. Yes, fall is a great time in the Leelanau.

The first snow can sometimes be a surprise. Drivers must relearn their "snow sense" and the plows must ready for their work ahead. The clouds hang long and deep and gray over the peninsula. Sometimes a foot of snow will drop in early November, as it often does, but the skiers, always ready, are anxious and already out to christen a new winter season. Though the warm earth usually melts the first snows, soon the county is covered in a white fairyland surrounded by beautiful blue waters to gaze at and admire.

The Essence of Timing . . .

First spring wildflowers: Mid-April. Trilliums blossom: Early to mid-May. Morel mushrooms: May. Cherry blossoms: Early to mid-May. Leaf-out of trees: Mid-May. Lake Michigan reaches seventy degrees: Late July to August. Meteor showers: Mid-August (most years). Coho salmon returns to rivers: September. Peak of fall colors: Second week of October. First snow: Varies from early November to mid-December.

. . . and perhaps you can add some of your own "essence" between the lines.

Whatever the season, the Leelanau is a most special part of the earth we share, an area to be guarded, appreciated, and loved.

The Essence of Leelanau

A Town-By-Town Guide In History

Leelinau, Leelinau
Daughter of Indian lore.
Are you among the wildflowers,
Or do you dance along the shore?

From a historical aspect the Leelanau contains interesting places and fact. Many of today's residents are third and fourth generation ancestors of those who previously lived here. This gives the Leelanau a kind of solidity uncommon in the world we share today. The information presented here barely scratches the surface of our legacy; it is up to us to preserve it. The intent of this chapter is to whet your appetite to want to discover more, by being here in Leelanau!

Leelanau, known as the "Land of Delight," has two explanations of its name. It was first named in 1840 by Henry Rowe Schoolcraft, United States Indian Commissioner. Earlier, Schoolcraft had compiled a group of legends that included "Leelinau, or the Lost Daughter, an Ojibwa Tale." This wistful maiden continually worried her family by often leaving home to spend time among the pines of a sylvan haunt called "Manitowak," or the sacred grove. On one of her visits she uttered a prayer to live "the life that spirits live." Her prayer was answered making this maiden leave home to live in her "Land of Delight," an enchanted "fairy haunted grove."

A more realistic version comes from the Michigan Department of State, which listed thumbnail descriptions of each county, Schoolcraft's romantic version was said to be completely erroneous. It was stated that the Ottawas and Ojibwas did not have the letter *L*. It claims that "Leelanau" was one of the pen names of Schoolcraft's wife.

Regardless of which explanation one wishes to believe, all sources agree on one thing—Leelanau was established as a county in 1863, and certainly is a "Land of Delight."

In the early 1800s Michigan territory was largely being overlooked by eastern pioneers migrating west. They were looking for fertile soils, and early surveys reported Michigan to be of sandy soils, swampy, and filled with Indians. Travel was difficult; the northern part of the state was accessible only by water. Its climate and the rugged forests did not hold much appeal to the farmers. Slowly, southern Michigan began to grow as fertile lands were discovered west of the port of Detroit and the Saginaw valley. Villages began to grow as schools, stores, and churches were needed to satisfy the growing white population.

In time, the north became populated by the white settlers. In 1855, there were yet no open roads in Leelanau. Some of the early settlers followed old Indian trails by foot or followed the beaches to get to Traverse City. In winter some traveled by ice. In 1862, word was out that a new road was being built from Newago all the way to Northport. Hearing that the new road was to be cut, Deacon Dame of Northport, at seventy years of age, started out on foot to examine this route. It took him two days. In 1870, a state road was laid out and thus began the secondary roads in the Leelanau. At that time going by road was slower than going by boat.

NORTHPORT

In the spring of 1849, Rev. George N. Smith led his group of Indians from the Holland area, taken over by the Dutch, to the north. Large tracts of lands in the north were ceded in exchange for lands in the southern part of the state. Moving north held greater appeal to the Indians than moving west, partly because for unaccountable years the Indians went annually to summer camps and villages in the north country.

Rev. George N. Smith arrived in Northport on June 12, 1849, aboard the schooner *Hiram Merrill,* along with a party of seventeen white men. They were accompanied by the Indians, who set out in canoes and Mackinaw boats. The only signs of civilization that they passed on this journey north were at Manistee and Grand Haven. Mr. Smith's four head of horses, rare in those days, were driven up the coast by four men. They had to ford streams and swamps and cut out brush in this wilderness where "the sound of an ax had never been heard."

First known as Waukazooville after the Indian who bought land from Chief Nagonaba's band of Indians, the town was soon to become the largest community in northwest Michigan for a time.

In 1851, Deacon Joseph Dame arrived and began constructing the first dock. By 1858, fifteen thousand cords of wood were sold to the steamers for fuel. Among the cargo shipped were apples, potatoes, hemlock bark (for tanning leather), fish, and pigeons.

The fish, though reduced in number, still survive. Much of the great forest gave way to orchards. The carrier pigeon was hunted to extinction. Reports state that there were "millions of pigeons" clouding up the sky. Trade with the pigeon, which began in New England in the 1600s, came west with the new settlers along with obvious greed. In 1736, these birds were sold in the marketplace for between seventy cents to one and one-half dollars per dozen. In 1875, nearly two and a half million birds were killed throughout the country. The last nesting sight in Leelanau was believed to be in 1877.

A favorite picnic spot for the old-time resident was at Northport Point, a spear of land extending into Grand Traverse Bay. The Indians called it "O-Ne-Ka-Win," or Carrying Point, because after crossing from Charlevoix to the present site of Northport, the Indians carried their canoes across the narrowest part of the peninsula, to save a few miles of paddling and avoid the rough water at the end of the point.

Today, Northport retains its nautical charm, attracting tourists, cottagers, and year-round residents alike, who enjoy some of the same things that the early Indians and first white men enjoyed.

GULL ISLAND

Gull Island lies offshore east of Northport. Early tax records referred to it as Ball, Trout, and Fisher Island. Early lake charts referred to it as Bellows Island. Residents have consistently called it Gull Island because of the large herring gulls that nest there every year. The gull population is directly related to the area industry. When the fishing business was thriving and the farmers had much of the area under cultivation, the gulls were happy, well fed, and plentiful. As the fishermen closed their businesses and farming began to change from vegetable to fruit orchard, the gull population decreased. The island is still a natural haven for the gulls, to be admired as they fly freely over the beautiful waters of the Leelanau.

OMENA or NEW MISSION POINT

Chief Ahgosa, a member of Rev. Peter Dougherty's mission at Old Mission Point, and members of his family first bought land after Indians were given the rights of citizenship and the rights to buy land.

Rev. Peter Dougherty followed Ahgosa in 1852, having moved from Old Mission to establish the Indian Mission at New Mission Point, today known as Omena. The Indians apparently gave Omena its name meaning "Is it so?", apparently a nickname given to Mr. Dougherty in his many conversations with the Indians.

In 1858, Mr. Dougherty built the Omena Presbyterian Church. The church is listed on the National Register of Historic Places under its historic name, Grove Hill New Mission Church.

SUTTONS BAY

The history of Suttons Bay began in 1854 when Harry C. Sutton with a crew of woodsmen settled on the bay and established camp so as to be able to supply fuel to the wood-burning steamboats on the Great Lakes. In 1867, Sutton platted an area there and called it Suttonsburg on the register of deeds. In 1871, Andrew Herbstrit, a missionary priest and real estate operator, platted six thousand lots and called it "Pleasant City," and it was during this decade that the name was changed to Suttons Bay.

The first industry in Suttons Bay was a gristmill, established in 1859 by Antoine Manseu, Jr. He bought the property from Chief Kenashu; it was three miles north of Suttons Bay at Bellanger Creek. In 1906, it was bought by Egging Bellanger. The building still stands.

Though the lumber era is past, Suttons Bay is home to one of the largest lumberyards in the Grand Traverse region. A sawmill was built on this site in the 1870s, later becoming an excelsior mill factory, owned by Carron and Diependbrock. The mill burned down in 1907. In 1914, Olaf Olsen and Charles Chadsey tore down a large building in Thomsonville (near Traverse City), and moved it to Suttons Bay by rail. The building was erected on the site and until 1944, operated as the Suttons Bay Planing Mill. The site is now home to Northern Lumber and Pro Hardware.

Another historic place alive today is the Bay Theatre. Originally it housed the Con Lather Blacksmith and the first volunteer fire department. In 1922, it became a general store; in 1946, the Bay Theatre, which it has been ever since. Today, it offers first-run and classic movies and live theater performances.

In 1879, Capt. J. C. Anderson brought bricks on his schooner from Milwaukee to build a new school. This replaced the original log house used for the school.

Local historian Helen Wransky recalls some of the past. Her great grandfather, John Hubert Duester, and her grandfather, John Duester, came to Leelanau in 1867. Helen's father, John Michael, was born here in 1885. Helen takes great pleasure in building a personal library of the history of Suttons Bay.

> Suttons Bay is very special to me. Through the years I have witnessed many changes. I felt as if I had the best of two worlds: I lived on a farm where it was quiet and peaceful, yet close to town, with the beautiful bay in our backyard.
>
> My memories are many and include: buying penny candy at the F. F. Smiseth Store; silent movies at the Colonial Theatre; school plays; high school graduation; rural mail delivery by horse and buggy with Lars Bolme and Paul Mork; party line telephones; seeing James Hendryx, local author of western stories, wearing his red plaid shirt

and Stetson hat; seeing my father get out at four a.m. to snowplow all the village sidewalks with a little old wood plow and a team of horses; homecomings in Suttons Bay featuring Heine and His Grenadiers from Milwaukee; hearing the noon whistle blow at the Peterson sawmill; getting potato vacation at school; hearing the fire whistle blow, then everyone asking Clara Lund at the telephone company "Where's the fire?"; seeing the old hitching posts on St. Joseph Street and the porches that hung out over the wooden walkways in front of the buildings, just like in the western movies. . . . Suttons Bay has been, and is, an interesting place.

LELAND

Leland, literally Lee-land, was called such by the sailors because of her natural harbor and protection from the strong winds. Several Indian tribes were her first inhabitants, borne out by the many relics found here, such as stone axes and flint arrowheads. There were many man-made mounds in the immediate area, possibly used as altars for sun worshipers. Leland was officially recognized in 1868.

The Indians called this spot "Mich-mi-go-bing," meaning, "the place to go where the canoes run up the river."

Antoine Manseau is credited as being the first white settler. He arrived in the spring of 1853. A sawmill was erected later that year. The power dam and powerhouse were both erected at the site of the sawmill on the Carp River. A larger dam was built in 1909, which raised the levels of North and South Lake Leelanau.

The 1860s through 1870s saw a booming population of nearly twenty-five hundred settlers because of the much-needed lumber industry. The lumber supply, near easy reach of water transportation, gradually exhausted itself. The lumber industry thus waned toward the end of the nineteenth century.

Indirectly created from the lumber industry was the manufacture of charcoal. Small steam-powered tugs hauled the charcoal along the river. In 1872, iron furnaces were built along the shores of Lake Michigan. Ore was brought from Escanaba, smelted by charcoal, and the iron shipped to southern markets.

The Women's Club was instrumental in helping Leland become a haven for artists. The club donated the W. T. Belt Building to Michigan State College (now Michigan State University) in 1939. The Belt Building is on the state register of Historic Places. Leland and the Leelanau Summer Art School have had a mutually rewarding relationship for more than fifty years.

FISHTOWN(on the waterfront of Leland)

Listed on the National Register of Historic Sites, Fishtown is a unique collection of shanties where fishing activities have been carried on since the mid-1800s. Many of the shanties live on as gift shops, having been restored to their original state. Adding to the authentic nautical charm, fishnets are hung, sea gulls encircle, and charter boats await passengers to carry on Lake Michigan.

The Leland River runs through the center of Fishtown, where it meets Lake Michigan. This river was called "Che-Mak-O-Ping" by the Indians, meaning "Bad Smell." At times, that title still fits! The fishing industry began before the turn of the century. One fishing business still in existence is Carlson's Fisheries. Nels Carlson, during a particularly bad winter, moved his family to Leland from North Manitou Island, where they had lived for several years. His four sons took up commercial fishing on the mainland in the early 1900s and the business is now run by Nel's grandson, Bill Carlson.

In 1918, a freight and mail service began between Fishtown (Leland) and the Manitou islands. Begun by J. Paetschow, it was later taken over by T. Grosvenor and is still run by the same family. They now offer passages and cruises along Lake Michigan and to North and South Manitou Island.

Fishtown really brings to life another time and season, and is a very popular attraction today.

LAKE LEELANAU

The village of Lake Leelanau has been called two previous names. The first was "Ke-ski-bi-ag," named by the Indians, meaning "Narrow body of water." Until the dam was built at Leland, raising the water level behind it, the stream that ran from south to north was narrow. In 1855, Simon and Jacob Schaub came to the narrows to farm and plant a vineyard; the name Provemont was given to the village. In the 1920s, the name was changed to Lake Leelanau, after the lake that rests on either side of town.

MAPLE CITY

Maple City was established in 1866. J. T. Sturtevent and his son came north from Ohio and bought several hundred acres of the maple timber. They built a factory to manufacture shoe pegs, thus at first the name Peg Town.

CEDAR

Established in 1892, Cedar has the distinction of being the newest town in Leelanau County. It was first known as Cedar City, having been named by the Sullivan Lumber Company, who erected a small shingle mill there because of the abundance of cedar trees.

Town-by-Town Guide in History

GLEN ARBOR AND EMPIRE

Julia Dickenson has provided the following information about Glen Arbor and Empire.

The name John is prominent in the settlement of the Glen Lake-Empire area of Leelanau County. John LaRue came from Chicago to South Manitou Island and then to the outlet of the Crystal River not far from what is now Glen Arbor. John E. Fisher who came from Wisconsin in the 1850s, bought a thousand acres of government land between Lake Michigan and Glen Lake (then called Bear Lake), and moved to acreage on Little Glen Lake after the Civil War.

Harriet McCart Fisher is credited with naming Glen Arbor for its woodland beauty. Lumbering and farming provided a livelihood for the settlers, as did fishing in Lake Michigan. Family farms provided food, but lumbering was a statewide industry that made use of local forests for cordwood supplied to the lake vessels, which stopped at the docks for fuel. Sawmills, gristmills, and docks were active places in the Glen Arbor area. Along with the Fishers, other early arrivals included Dr. William Walker from Wisconsin, who established a cranberry marsh south of the village and planted an apple orchard with many varieties of the fruit. D. H. Day was also among the prominent names in the early days.

English, Dutch, German, and Norwegian names still abound in the area, and descendants of these families are proud of their heritage.

Empire, in the southwest corner of Leelanau County, had the largest sawmill in the county in the late 1800s and early 1900s. It was a thriving village of one thousand people who lived here during the lumbering days. The first settler was John LaRue, who originally came from Chicago about 1847 to South Manitou Island; he later settled at the mouth of the Crystal River on Lake Michigan, and then permanently in the region that became known as Empire.

The name of the village is believed to have come from the *Empire,* a lake vessel stranded on ice near the Sleeping Bear sand dunes. It is said that the vessel became the first school in the area.

The early settlers farmed, worked in the mills, set up businesses, and cut timber from nearby forests. The cherry industry took hold after the forests were cut, and for many years, migrant workers came to the area during the harvest season. Cherry farming has become largely mechanized, and only a few accommodations for migrant workers remain.

In 1950, the U.S. government established an early warning system, and airmen assigned to the air base were present for many years. Some of them stayed in the area and reared their families after the base closed.

A relative newcomer to the area is the National Park Service, which established the Sleeping Bear Dunes National Lakeshore in the early 1970s.

MUSEUMS

EMPIRE HERITAGE GROUP (616) 326-5568 or 5181. P.O. Box 192, Empire, MI 49630. The Empire Heritage Group was formed in 1978 to preserve Empire's past. The museum has many interesting features, such as the Roen Saloon, a turn-of-the-century watering hole for the lumbermen, and a parlor-kitchen-sewing room, featuring all the convenience the year 1900 had to offer. There are also artifacts from a nearby ghost town, Norway Town, a mill workers settlement. There is a railroad exhibit and a blacksmith and barn display.

Behind the museum, nestled in the woods, you will discover a one-room schoolhouse. The building serves as an audiovisual center, where various programs are available daily.

A museum store features a fine collection of cards and reproduction toys, as well as museum and local publications.

LEELANAU HISTORICAL MUSEUM (616) 256-7475. 203 E. Cedar Street, Leland, MI 49654. Operated by the Leelanau Historical Society and founded in 1957. It is housed next to the Leland Township Public Library. Exhibit themes change yearly.

More than just an exhibit hall, the museum strives to preserve and promote the heritage of Leelanau. This is accomplished through a collection and conservation of many artifacts, interpretive exhibits, and educational programs. There are various hands-on activities for both the student and the young at heart.

The story of the settling and developing of the county unravels as you walk through the halls of the exhibits. Discover Leelanau's rich maritime history, learn about shipwrecks in the Manitou passage, and of the archeological findings. Learn about the work being done to unfold these past legacies.

There is an archives for historical and genealogical research. Great effort is being made to preserve, also, the oral history of some of Leelanau's old-time residents, documenting the times and seasons of Leelanau's past.

SLEEPING BEAR POINT COAST GUARD MARITIME MUSEUM. See chapter 8.

GRAND TRAVERSE LIGHTHOUSE FOUNDATION. See chapter 8.

The Native Americans

Birch-bark canoe silently
Touches shore,
Bringing Anishinabe, "First Man."
Followed by many more.

Suffice it to say that it was not the French explorers, in the early 1600s, nor other white men that first settled in the Leelanau. The title goes to the native American Indian who lived and hunted in the Northwest Territory. There is direct evidence of occupation from about forty-seven hundred years ago during the late Archaic period (3000 B.C. to 500 B.C.), at least that the area was used periodically. Andrew J. Blackbird was instrumental in recalling some of this past in *History of the Ottawa* and *Chippewa Indians of Michigan: A Grammar of Their Language and Personal Family History,* which he wrote in 1887. Also known as Mack-aw-de-be-nessy (Black Hawk), he wrote that there were "many other Indians in this region prior to the occupancy by the Ottawa and Chippewa . . . who have long ago gone out of existence. Not a page of their history is on record; but only an allusion to them in our traditions."

Not much is written of the early history of the Ottawa and Chippewa, for much was passed on orally by tradition. According to Blackbird, their "legends resemble Bible History; particularly the legends with regard to the Great Flood, which has been in our language for many centuries and the legend of the Great Fish who swallowed the prophet Ne-Naw-Bo-Zhoo, who came out alive again." As for the flood, he continues: "The Legends say it was caused . . . by the great Ne-Naw-Bo-Zhoo. . . . No great ark . . . but a great canoe which he entered with his animals and floated."

It is interesting that the Indians (later at times condemned and called "savages"), according again to Blackbird, "had great moral precepts or moral commandments by which the Ottawa and Chippewa nations of Indians were governed in their primitive state, were almost the same as the ten commandments. . . . There were about twenty other 'uncivilized' precepts. . . . The first precept; Thou Shalt fear Thy Great Creator, who is the Ruler of all things. . . . The sixth; Honor thy Father and thy Mother that thy days may be long upon the land."

The Ottawa and Chippewa, based far to the north in Upper Michigan and Ontario, lived in a transitional ecological zone between the mild climate and hardwood forest to the south and the colder conifer climate to the north.

Their camps were temporary, used as hunting camps seasonally. The Indian way of life demanded this mobility, because of several contributing influences. These included fear of hostile tribes, a short harvest period, and infertile soils. The great conifer forests provided few food-yielding plants for them. They did not hunt the same location each year.

As for survival, the Indians spent much of the year living in small groups, hunting game, and gathering wild plants. Maple trees, tapped for syrup, were relied on substantially as a food source.

The Chippewa (Ojibwa) hunted with bow and arrow, trapped, snared, and fished. They were not farmers, but harvested wild rice, a ritual taught to the small ones that lasted the rest of their lives.

The Native Americans

During late summer to early fall there was enough food in one location for these groups to join in large villages on the lakeshore near their fisheries. In late fall, when all the fish were stored, they once again divided into smaller family groups for the winter hunt. During preparations for the first hunt, offerings were given to the hunters' "Manitou," or guardian spirit, with ritual dance and song.

Domesticated crops, especially corn, were extremely important to the lifeways of the Ottawa (Odawa) and Chippewa (Ojibwa) of the region. Late spring through early winter, a stable food supply could be assured. By late winter game was not easy to catch. The plant and fish foods that they would preserve often were eaten or spoiled before spring. Corn was the staple that they came to rely on, for it was the

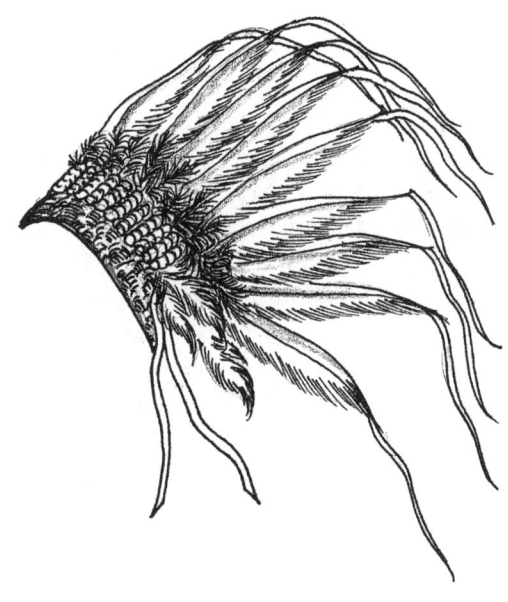

The Native Americans

source that could be preserved through the leanest months of the year.

The Ottawa, or Odawa (name meaning "to trade" or "people who trade"), traveled with loaded canoes and traded corn, tobacco, and woven mats for pottery, paints, and dyes.

The Chippewa, or Ojibwa, called themselves "Anishinabe" (meaning first man). According to legend, the two tribes were brothers, the Ottawa the eldest. Again, according to Blackbird, "every tribe of Indians has a different "coat of arms" or symbolic sign by which they are known to one another. The emblem of the Ottawa is a moose and for the Chippewa, a sea gull."

Before the white man arrived, there were a few scattered Indian villages in the Leelanau peninsula. Used as summer homes for many years, these were near the lakeshore. The inland was used little, except for a few trails to other villages and to the meadows and lakes for hunting and fishing. Sad to say when the white man did come, he came as foreigner and took what he wanted, forcing the first settlers to come to his terms rather than vice versa. The Indians were culturally scattered across the land; what chance did they have against this new, centrally located force?

"Even the word Michigan," according to Blackbird, "is an Indian name, which we pronounce 'Mi-chi-gum', and simply means 'Monstrous Lake.'" So to this day their hold on Michigan is a strong one indeed.

In 1836, the government confirmed the right of the Ottawa and Chippewa to own and occupy millions of acres of land. Under this treaty several "in common" reservations were set aside exclusively for them. But of the Treaty of 1836, Blackbird states:

> [M]y people—the Ottawas and the Chippewas—were unwilling parties, but they were compelled to sign, blindly and ignorant of the true spirit of the treaty and the true import of some of its conditions. They thought when signing the treaty that they were securing reservations of lands... as permanent homes for themselves and their children in the future, but before six months had elapsed... they were told by their white neighbors that their reservations of land

would expire in five years, instead of being perpetual as they believed. . . . At this time they would be compelled to leave their homes, and if they refused they would be driven at the point of a bayonet. . . . At this . . . more than half of my people fled into Canada. . . to the protection of the British government. . . even before receiving a single copper of the promised annuities.

Between the Treaty of 1836 and 1855, a new migration to the Grand Traverse region began in 1849 with the move of the Waw-ka-zoo, or Black River Band, of Ottawas. They settled in a new village near Northport.

In 1852, another band under Chief Pe-shaw-be moved south from Cross Village (north of Petoskey). This band built Eagleton, today known as Peshawbestown. The town was named after its then ruling chief. From 1895 on, it came to be known by its present name.

In 1848, Rev. George Nelson Smith arrived on an exploratory trip. He wrote: "All agree to join our mission. They talked well but all agree to buy on the lake shore, not on the shore of Grand Traverse." But much of the land set aside for the Indians in the Treaty of 1855 never made it into the Indians' hands. At Grand Traverse, for example, more than 25,640 acres of the 87,000 reserved acres were excluded from Indian settlement by federal laws. Selections made before 1857 were not registered with the federal government because of the now familiar ring of bureaucratic mix-ups. Finally, when they were registered with the proper office, many of the better parcels chosen were no longer available! Even when they did take title to land, it was often not for long. There was much fraud, and many Indians lost their land to trespassers. They did not have the tradition of farming and would leave for a while, and someone else would move in. To the native American, land was held "in common." To take their land and slice it up in sections, giving "title" to their land was foreign to them. It could be compared to us today as slicing up the air we breathe, giving title to it in sections as ours and ours alone. Totally inconceivable! The concept of private ownership began in feudal England, was brought to the Americas, and then forced upon the native Americans.

A century later, many lost their homes to unpaid taxes, another slap in the face to an old way being forced into this new monetary way of change. In 1878, the Northwest Ordinance for the government of the Northwest Territory had provided that these lands, held in trust, be tax exempt.

Late in the 1930s, Leelanau County Prosecutor Emelia Schaub and Circuit Court Judge Parm Gilbert agitated to have the county held in trust for the Indians. The band in 1943 was given deed to two hundred acres of land (including a 12½-acre reservation in Peshawbestown). The Grand Traverse Band of Ottawa and Chippewa was given federal recognition to the land in 1980.

Today the Grand Traverse Band of Ottawa and Chippewa Indians has acclimated itself to present-day life. An interim tribal chairman of the band spoke of this change: "We're talking about survival. You have to be able to adapt to the dominant society in order to survive [as a people]. You have to make their ways work for you." Giving testament to their survival is the Grand Traverse Band's Tribal Center, with its casino, 450-seat Bingo Palace, 52-room GTB motel, and an Indian Art Store and gift shop. In the heart of Peshawbestown, the casino opened in 1985. In 1991, a 13,500-square-foot casino was opened. For the tribe, it brings a stable economic base.

These new ways adopted out of necessity have not made the old ways forgotten. Today, many of the young people are harboring an interest in their past of long ago. If Indians seem reluctant to talk about some of these old ways, the outsider is expected to understand that potential to exploit exists. The white man must understand this and not trespass upon the Indians' commitment to their heritage and rightfully deserved privacy.

Leelanau Lodging

Leelanau, Leelanau, Land of such delight.
Once coming here, to such revered land
Will not let her for long
Out of one's heart or sight.

From small country inn to major resort, Leelanau can accommodate! Some of the state's nicest lodging facilities can be found here. Couple that with the area's bountiful beauty and you have quite a combination.

Many establishments are open year-round, especially so with skiing ever growing in popularity; however, please call ahead for this as well as price-per-night information. We do not list prices, but a general description with three price categories. These are based on double occupancy and during peak season.

Inexpensive: under $50 per night
Moderate: $50 to $85 per night
Expensive: over $85 per night

Leelanau Lodging

TRAVERSE CITY(that part in Leelanau County)

TALL SHIP MALABAR, "Floating Bed and Breakfast" (see chapter 10)
WINDJAMMMER BEACH RESORT (616) 946-7442. 11998 S. West-Bay Shore Drive, Traverse City, MI 49654. This nice resort is on five wooded acres two miles from downtown Traverse City on M-22. There are two sandy beaches, one on Cedar Lake and one on West Grand Traverse Bay. There are fifteen furnished cottages. Amenities include a large hot tub. (See also chapter 11.)

SUTTONS BAY

RED LION MOTOR LODGE (616) 271-6694. 5100 S. West-Bay Shore Drive, Suttons Bay, MI 49684. Enjoy quiet country atmosphere at this rustic and charming lodge, located twelve miles from Traverse City. There are 150 feet of beach frontage on West Grand Traverse Bay facing Lee Point. Single and double rooms, efficiency units, and town house units with spiral staircases. Inexpensive to moderate.
LEE POINT INN Bed and Breakfast (616) 271-6770. 2885 S. Lee Point Lane, Suttons Bay, MI 49682. A beautiful traditional home with a private beach on West Grand Traverse Bay. Fabulous setting! From here you look out over the Old Mission peninsula, and at night you can see Traverse City's twinkling lights. Three bedrooms, each overlooking the bay. Delicious breakfast served on the deck by the beach. Moderate.
MORNING GLORY BEACH BED AND BREAKFAST (616) 271-6047. 378 N. Stony Point Road, Suttons Bay, MI 49682. Enjoy memorable sunsets, floral gardens, and relaxing afternoons on the beach. Located on serene Stony Point peninsula, this charming home features a cottage-type atmosphere with a private suite, and continental "plus" breakfast. Expensive.

CHATEAU REEF CLUB AND RESORT (616) 271-3634. P.O. Box 295, Suttons Bay, MI 49682. The Chateau Reef is fifteen miles north of Traverse City on beautiful Suttons Bay. The extraordinary view feasts your eye on four counties and the breadth of Grand Traverse Bay. All decorator-appointed units face the safe, sandy beach. The building itself is beautifully designed and blends in with the beach and surrounding countryside. There are studio, one- and two- bedroom apartments, some with kitchens. Expensive.

OPEN WINDOWS BED AND BREAKFAST (616) 271-4300. 613 St. Marys Avenue, Suttons Bay, MI 49682. A Victorian farmhouse in the village of Suttons Bay. Beautifully furnished with family heirlooms. Outdoors there is a lovely front porch filled

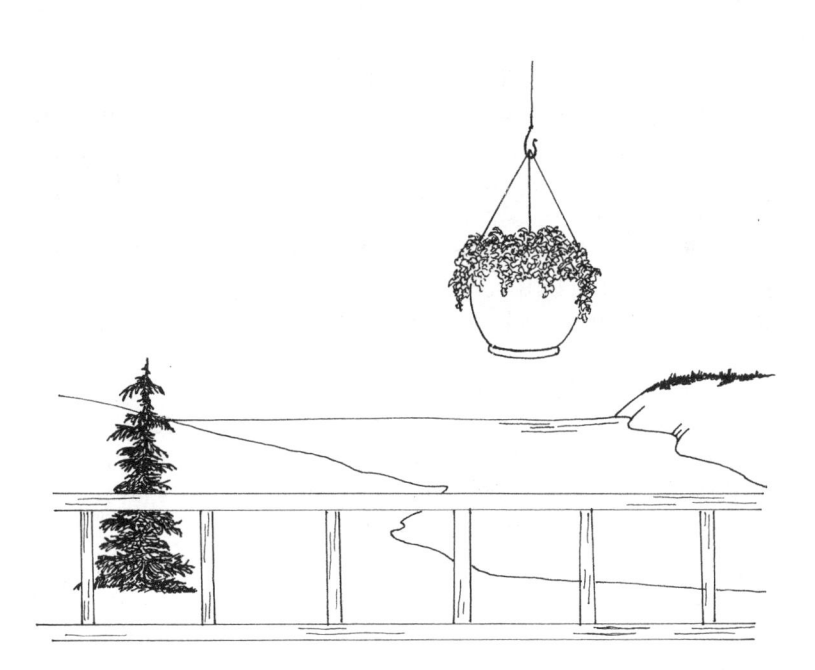

Leelanau Lodging

with wicker and a gazebo. Continental "plus" breakfast. Moderate.

WAYSIDE MOTEL (616) 271-3636. M-22. Suttons Bay, MI 49682. Just south of the village of Suttons Bay. Small, comfortable, no-frills rooms. Open year-round. Inexpensive.

GTB MOTEL (616) 271-6330. P.O. Box 717, Suttons Bay, MI 49682. Twenty miles north of Traverse City on M-22. This motel is owned and operated by the Grand Traverse Band of Ottawa and Chippewa Indians. There are fifty-one immaculate, well-appointed units, which overlook the Leelanau Sands Casino, Super Bingo Place, and Indian Art Store. Moderate.

NORTHPORT

THE HOMEWOOD (616) 386-5831. M-22, Northport, MI 49670. Completely furnished, spic and span cottages with kitchenettes. Laundromat on premises. The village and beach with lifeguard are within walking distance. Inexpensive to moderate (also see camping in chapter 11).

SUNRISE LANDING RESORT/MOTEL (616) 386-5010. 6530 N. Manitou Trail, Northport, MI 49670. On eight acres overlooking the waters of Northport Bay in a secluded, landscaped setting. Many homey touches complement these eight units, some with kitchenettes. One hundred fifty feet of sandy beach. Moderate.

THE OLD MILL POND INN BED AND BREAKFAST (616) 386-7341. 202 West 3d Street, Northport, MI 49670. The house, built in 1895, is furnished with interesting antiques and museum-like pieces, comfortably arranged. Eccentric and eclectic can only describe this place. Extensive gardens, including a formal Italian garden with roaming peacocks in summer. Breakfast served on a big wraparound screened porch filled with white wicker furniture. Moderate.

TALL SHIP MANITOU BED AND BREAKFAST. Spectacular three- and six-day windjammer cruises (see chapter 10).

NORTHSHORE INN (616) 386-7111. 12271 N. Northport Point Road, Northpoint, MI 49670. Luxury bed and breakfast right on a sandy beach of Grand Traverse Bay. Elegant spacious home built in 1946 in the colonial tradition. The rooms each have a private bath and fireplace. Outdoor Jacuzzi, porches, and decks. Gourmet breakfasts. Afternoon aperitifs. This must be one of the best bed and breakfasts in Leelanau, if not the Midwest. Expensive.

LELAND (including Fishtown)

THE LELAND LODGE (616) 256-9848. P.O. Box 344, 565 Pearl Street, Leland, MI 49654. "At the very top of Leland," nestled among tall pine and oak. Distinctive, carefully appointed guest rooms and efficiency apartments. Elegant dining on premises (see chapter 5). Lake or golf course views are available. Moderate to expensive.

THE RIVERSIDE INN (616) 256-9971. P.O. Box 1012, 302 River Street, Leland, MI 49654. Lovely restored inn on the Leland River. An elegant, yet comfortable atmosphere. Fantastic gourmet breakfasts (see chapter 5). Moderate to expensive.

FALLING WATERS LODGE (616) 256-9832. P.O. Box 345, Leland, MI 49654. Overlooking Fishtown and on the Leland River. It's a charmingly romantic spot within earshot of the waterfall's delightful sounds. Just a short walk to a sandy Lake Michigan beach and marina. Accommodations offer guest rooms, loft, executive suites, and penthouse. All rooms face water. Expensive.

MANITOU MANOR BED AND BREAKFAST (616) 256-7712. P.O. Box 864, Leland, MI 49654. Three miles south of Leland on M-22. Turn-of-the-century farmhouse, completely refurbished. Traditional furnishings, huge living room with natural stone fireplace. All rooms with private baths. Delightful breakfasts with offerings, such as homemade applesauce, stewed rhubarb and strawberries, and oatmeal-cinnamon pancakes—all locally grown products. Surrounded by cherry orchards and woods. Within walking distance of a winery and farm market. Moderate.

JOLLI LODGE (616) 256-9291. 29 N. Manitou Trail, Lake Leelanau, MI 49653. Three miles south of Leland, on the shore of Lake Michigan. Idyllic old-time setting. Lodge rooms available by the night. Fifteen housekeeping cottages and apartments by the week. Badminton, Ping-Pong, pocket billiards, shuffleboard, horseshoes, and tennis court. An excellent family-type resort. Moderate.

LAKE LEELANAU

FOUNTAIN POINT (616) 256-9800. 1008 S. Lake Leelanau Drive, Lake Leelanau, MI 49653. Historic landmark established in 1889, making it the county's oldest family summer resort. About 1860, French fur trader Andre de Beloit attempted to drill for oil on this piece of land. Instead of oil, he struck a gusher of sparkling water at a depth of nine hundred feet that has flowed since 1863. All sixteen cottages have a view of the historic fountain. Guest rooms in main house. Sandy beach, tennis courts, shuffleboard, volleyball, and rowboats. Continental breakfast. Moderate.

CENTENNIAL INN (616) 271-6460. 7251 E. Alpers Road, Lake Leelanau, MI 49653. A centennial farm, restored to its 1865 charm and warmth. Furnished with country antiques, large country kitchen with woodstove, cozy dining room, parlor. Four-poster beds with antique quilts and coverlets. Continental "plus" breakfast. Moderate.

TRAPPER'S COVE (616) 256-7263. 1851 S. Lakeshore Drive, Lake Leelanau, MI 49653. Intimate, two- and three-bedroom cottages on the shores of South Lake Leelanau. Each unit furnished with television, fourteen-foot boat, and docking facilities. Excellent beach for children. Weekly rates. Moderate.

CEDAR HAVEN COTTAGE (616) 256-9294. P.O. Box 966, Lake Leelanau, MI 49653. Family-operated resort in restful setting on North Lake Leelanau. Cedar log cottages have screened porches and fully equipped kitchens. Each cottage is on the shoreline in a wooded area and comes equipped with a fourteen-foot boat and several moorings in deeper water. Excellent sand beach, dock, swim float, and evening beach fires. Weekly rates in summer. Moderate.

CEDAR

SUGAR LOAF RESORT (800) 748-0117 or (616) 228-5461. 4500 Sugar Loaf Mountain Road, Cedar, MI 49621-9755. Nestled among the rolling hills lies Sugar Loaf Resort, catering year-round to the many tourists who flock here. Accommodations include lodge rooms, town houses, and winged-foot condominiums. Lodge rooms have either two double beds or a queen-sized bed and a double sleeper sofa. Town houses are available as two- and four-bedroom units featuring a fireplace, dining area, and kitchen. The condominiums are designed studio, one- and two-bedroom units, each with a two-person whirlpool tub. The resort offers attractive packages; call for brochure. Emphasis is on year-round activities, including golf, skiing, biking, and other family activities. Three pools, one indoor and two outdoor. Moderate to expensive. Corporate and family rates available.

MAPLE CITY

LEELANAU COUNTRY INN (616) 228-5060. 149 E. Harbor Highway, Maple City, MI 49664. On M-22, eight miles south of Leland. This lovely inn was established in 1890 and features true country atmosphere. There is a comfortable commons area for guests to share. Outside enjoy spectacular gardens that the owner lovingly tends. Full service restaurant (see chapter 5). Moderate to expensive.

PAUL'S PARADISE (616) 228-7100. 351 E. Harbor Highway, Maple City, MI 49664. On Little Traverse Lake. Each unit has two bedrooms and fireplace. Open year-round. Moderate.

Leelanau Lodging

GLEN ARBOR AND EMPIRE; "Sleeping Bear Country"

THE HOMESTEAD (616) 334-5000. M-22, Glen Arbor, MI 49636. "America's Freshwater Resort" and one of it's nicest. On Lake Michigan in a wooded acreage adjacent to the National Park. Choose a lodge room, a suite, or a one- to four-bedroom condominium. Registered guests enjoy access to a golf academy, tennis, boating, three pools and two spa pools, and children's program. Miles of beautiful sand beach to walk and view fabulous sunsets. Downhill and cross-country skiing (see chapter 11). Expensive.

GLEN ARBOR BED AND BREAKFAST (616) 334-6789. 6548 Western Avenue, Glen Arbor, MI 49636. This 1877 farmhouse is ideally situated in the heart of Glen Arbor. Main house, graced by congenial hosts Mike and Becky Sutherland, offers a magnificent stone fireplace, wood floors, and antique furnishings. Two cottages, adjacent to the main house, offer the same charming comfort with stone fireplaces and knotty pine paneling. Continental plus. Moderate to expensive.

GLEN CRAFT MARINA AND RESORT (616) 334-4556. 6391 Lake Street, Glen Arbor, MI 49636. Modern cottages on the sandy north shore of Glen Lake. Marina facilities (see chapter 10). The resort is on three acres of property within walking distance of Glen Arbor. Moderate.

GLEN CRAFT VILLAS (616) 334-3969. 6375 Lake Street, Glen Arbor, MI 49636. On Glen Lakes north shore and offers one- to four-bedroom housekeeping villas. Amenities include fireplace, ceiling fans, tennis court, shuffleboard, sauna, swim raft, and marina facilities. Moderate.

THE SYLVAN INN (616) 334-4333. P.O. Box 648, Glen Arbor, MI 49636. Two blocks west of the stop sign on M-109. Established in 1885, this registered Landmark Inn began as a respite for lumbermen and mariners alike. Today, over a hundred years later, this inn brings you the same gracious country charm. Luxuriously restored yet retains its historic ambience and flavor. Sauna, whirlpool. Continental "plus" breakfast. Moderate to expensive.

GLEN ARBOR LAKESHORE INN (616) 334-3773. M22, Glen Arbor, MI 49636. Comfortable accommodations in the village, 1½ blocks to Lake Michigan. Moderate.

CLIPPER HOUSE INN (616) 326-5518. 10085 Front Street, Empire, MI 49630. A quaint bed and breakfast above a country store/restaurant. Read the interesting guest register displayed with shows signatures from the world over. Just a short walk to Lake Michigan. Full breakfast buffet. Moderate.

EMPIRE HOUSE BED AND BREAKFAST (616) 326-5524. 11015 Lacore, Empire, MI 49630. This 1890s farmhouse is in a quiet country setting complete with large wraparound porch. Four rooms with private outside entrances. Continental "plus" breakfast. Moderate.

MAPLE LANE RESORT (616) 334-3413. 8720 Dorsey Road, Empire, MI 49630. In the heart of Sleeping Bear country, this has to be one of the nicest motels in Leelanau. The twenty-two units have been carefully and lovingly remodeled. The combination office and parlor is charming. Family-owned and operated, it offers guests that special touch of friendliness. Rooms, kitchenettes, and apartments. Private beach on west side of Glen Lake with sun deck, dock, and boat moorings. Canoes and rowboats. Picnic tables, grills, fire pit, and outdoor games. Recreation room. Continental breakfast. Moderate.

SHADY SHORES RESORT (616) 334-3252. 7121 West County Road 616, Empire, MI 49630. Ten cottages on Glen Lake. The one-, two-, or three-bedroom cottages are completely furnished, and include kitchen, television, and outdoor furniture. The cottages are on a traffic free-commons area, amid birch, pine, and hardwood. Rowboats, dock, boat moorings, picnic tables, fire pit, and horseshoes. By day, week, or month. Open year-round. Moderate.

LAKESHORE INN (616) 326-5145. M-22, Empire, MI 49630. Twelve-unit motel with comfortable accommodations. Just a short walk to Lake Michigan and South Bar Lake beaches. Moderate.

WHITE GULL INN BED AND BREAKFAST (616) 334-4486 P.O. Box 351, Glen Arbor, MI 49636 Comfortable family atmosphere,

Leelanau Lodging

known for special "homey" touches. Breakfast served in big country kitchen and includes homemade jams, jellies, and bake goods. Moderate.

GLEN EDEN RESORT (616) 334-3671. 4615 Northwoods Road, Glen Arbor, MI 49636. A family-owned tradition on Glen Lake. Meals are included in rates. Moderate.

DUNE VALLEY MOTEL (616) 334-3789. On M-109, Glen Arbor, MI 49636. Attractive air-conditioned rooms near the beaches. Inexpensive to moderate.

5

Dining, Leelanau-Style

Leelanau, Leelanau,"Land of Delight." Lake Michigan breezesBring such an appetite!Dining in the Leelanau is really different! There are no fast-food franchises in the county, unlike most tourist destinations. Instead, chefs lure you by their fresh ideas and local ingredients, prepared Leelanau-style.

Your dining tour starts at the base of the Leelanau, in Traverse City at S. West-Bay Shore Drive (M-22, designated Lake Michigan Scenic Circle Tour) and Traverse Highway (M-72). Following the scenic shore of West Grand Traverse Bay, M-22 will take you into the very pretty town of Suttons Bay. Next stops are tranquil Omena and nautical Northport near the tip of the little finger peninsula. Heading south you enter Leland and Fishtown, a quaint, historic community on Lake Michigan and a wharf. Taking a short side trip, southeast of Leland, take E. Duck Lake Rd. (M-204) to the quiet little village of Lake Leelanau. Now go back south heading along Lake Michigan (M-22) toward the magnificent dunes and Glen Arbor with a few side treks into Maple City and Cedar. Next is Empire and finally, heading back east (M-72) toward Traverse City, Burdickville—two special places.
Dinners: Inexpensive: $8 and under

Dining, Leelanau Style

Moderate: $8 to $16
Expensive: over $16
Most establishments serve alcohol.

TRAVERSE CITY

SWEITZER'S BY THE BAY (616) 947-0493. 13890 S. West-Bay Shore Drive. Established since 1977, this is a great family restaurant. There is a lovely open feeling with large windows overlooking West Grand Traverse Bay. The food is consistently well prepared, with unique items such as "chicken charlie" and "Aunt Betty's scramble." Fantastic array of shrimp and chicken dishes. Children's menu, senior citizen discount, cocktails. Open for breakfast, lunch, and dinner seven days year-round. Inexpensive to moderate.

GEPPETO'S ON THE BAY (616) 947-7079. 13641 S. West-Bay Shore Drive. Authentic Italian dining. Casual and affordable. Appetizers, salads, pasta, beef, and chicken. Beautiful view of West Bay. Outside dining and docking facilities. Cocktails. Year-round. Moderate.

SCOTT'S HARBOR GRILLE (616) 922-2114. 12719 S. West-Bay Shore Drive. A fun place to dine for lunch or dinner, or just to gather with friends for a drink. In summer enjoy a beautiful deck overlooking the marina for outside dining. A popular place year-round. Great casual dining with some exciting dinner menu changes plus items such as conch fritters, buffalo chips, "awesome" burgers. Docking facilities. Inexpensive.

WINDOWS (616) 941-0100. 7677 S. West-Bay Shore Drive. Extremely well known for distinctive gourmet foods served with unique presentation. Established since 1986, one of the finest restaurants in the north. Choices include veal Wynn Dixie, rack of lamb, and the finest in soups and salads. Specializes in desserts, especially chocolates, such as Chocolate Mousse Olivia. Prix fixe. Children's menu. Lower level offers lighter fare. Outdoor deck over the bay. Docking facilities. Open year-round. Moderate to expensive.

THE HAYLOFT INN (616) 941-0832. 5100 W. M-72. Hearty fare including Mexican specialties, chicken, perch, smelt, and sandwiches. Cozy, country-antique atmosphere. Inexpensive.

SUTTONS BAY

PEPELLASHI'S SILVER SWAN (616) 271-4100. 1381 S. West-Bay Shore Drive. Established since 1985 this fine family restaurant features authentic European dining in a light and airy setting. They serve breakfast, lunch, and dinner. Some of their specialties include fresh German potato pancakes, homemade soups, and fresh bread baked daily. Dinner choices include fresh lake trout, and Wiener schnitzel. The Pepellashis tend a garden out back for special summer freshness. Open year-round. Moderate.

BOONE'S PRIME TIME (616) 271-6688. 102 St. Joseph Street. Serving food and spirits, this family-owned and operated restaurant was established in 1980 by the Boone family, natives of the area. The restaurant is rustic, fashioned from timbers from the family farm and structured around a blazing stone fireplace, radiating warmth and coziness. A "fatal attraction" is their award-winning Booneburger, made from ground steak and charbroiled to order. Their motto is "The best quali-

Dining, Leelanau Style

ty and largest quantity at a very reasonable price," and they live up to it! The atmosphere is charming and friendly and top quality service is provided, making this a wonderful and memorable dining experience. Open year-round. Inexpensive to moderate.

HATTIE'S (616) 271-6222. 111 St. Joseph Street. Elegant gourmet dining noted for being one of the best in the state. For a truly unique meal, give this place a try. Great appetizers, great dining. Sample sautéed mushroom ravioli with morel mushrooms, cracked crust pizza with roasted peppers. They make ordinary pork chops into the extraordinary by marinating, grilling, and serving with a tart cherry sauce. Menu changes. Call ahead for theater menu specials. Moderate to expensive.

HOSE HOUSE DELI (616) 271-6303. 303 St. Joseph Street. This historic firehouse was built in 1913. In 1985, it was converted into a deli-style restaurant with lots of great items on the menu. Special homemade soups and chili, delicious sandwiches, beef gyros, veggie pitas, salads. They offer round and square deep-dish pizzas in the evening. Fridays and Saturdays are Greek nights with choices such as flaming cheese saganaki, moussaka, dolmades, and souvlakia. Open year-round. Inexpensive to moderate.

EDDIE'S VILLAGE INN (616) 271-3300. 201 St. Joseph Street. Historic inn built in 1871 by F. J. Fetch, and operated as the Union House until 1879. It was next purchased by a retired sea captain, J. C. Anderson. Born in Norway, he skippered sailing ships until his retirement in 1879. He is credited with bringing in the bricks for the new Suttons Bay school, which was built to replace the original log cabin. It is one of the oldest continuously operating inns in the Grand Traverse region. Its current owners, the Rothgarbers, have owned the inn since 1956. There are two sides, one for dining and the other for that old-time bar atmosphere. Come meet their first lady bartender in over 120 years. Eddie's serves breakfast, lunch, and dinner, featuring standbys such as hamburgers, steaks, and pizza. It's a favorite gathering for locals, as it has been for over a century. Open year-round. Inexpensive to moderate.

THE ROMAN WHEEL (616) 271-4176. 116 St. Joseph Street

(next to the bank). Excellent pizzas, subs, broasted chicken, and salads. Dine in or take out. Deck. Open year-round. Inexpensive.
    CAPPUCCINO'S CAFÉ (616) 271-CAFE (2233). 102 Broadway (near post office). A gourmet coffeehouse extraordinaire. Features espresso, cappucino, and other fine coffees. Decadent pastries and desserts. Full breakfast and lunch menu. Patio. Dine in or take out. Inexpensive.

OMENA

    HARBOR BAR AND MARINA (616) 386-5388. On M-22. From here the view is terrific over lovely Omena Bay. Summers enjoy your favorite sandwich and beverage on the deck. Offering ground round burgers, chicken, and shrimp. Docking facilities, sixteen slips. Open year-round. Closed Mondays. Inexpensive.

NORTHPORT

    THE BEECH TREE CAFÉ (616) 386-5200. 202 Waukazoo. A summer café at the Beech Tree Craft Gallery. They offer soups, salads, and sandwiches. A pleasant midday stop for lunch, dessert, cappuccino, or homemade lemonade. Inexpensive.
    THE LITTLE FINGER RESTAURANT (616) 386-5281. 108 Waukazoo. A summertime family establishment, serving breakfast, lunch, and dinner. Country fried chicken, fresh lake perch, and Lake Michigan whitefish are some of their specialties. The salad bar features over thirty items. Inexpensive to moderate.
    STUBB'S (616) 386-7611. 115 Waukazoo. Reestablished in 1990, Stubb's is a year-round favorite for locals and visitors. Summertime enjoy relaxed dining on the screened porch outdoors. Year-round, call for times. Inexpensive to moderate.

Dining, Leelanau Style

THE LIGHTHOUSE COFFEE SHOP (616) 386-7321. 215 Mill Street. In the Harbor Haus. A charming spot for breakfast, lunch, or coffee break. Fresh baked goods. Lunch features homemade soups and sandwiches. The owners are congenial and fussy. Inexpensive.

SHIP'S GALLEY PIZZERIA (616) 386-5701. 119 Nagonaba. Terrific homemade pizzas and fresh sandwiches. Hand-dipped ice cream. Inexpensive.

THE WILLOWBROOK (616) 386-5617. 201 Mill Street. Great hamburgers, New York-style deli sandwiches, homemade candies, pies, and popcorn. They take pride in being a truly authentic ice cream parlor. Delicious pizza too! Inexpensive.

WOODY'S SETTLING INN (616) 386-9933. 116 Waukazoo. Their motto is "Life is serious but food is fun!" They have served Northport for well over a decade and a half with pastas, steaks, and seafood. Foods accent a New Orleans flavor with a New Orleans chef. Moderate.

HAPPY HOUR TAVERN (616) 386-9923. 7900 N. Manitou Trail (halfway between Northport and Leland at the foot of Gill's Pier). Since 1936, this former General Store has served locals and visitors as the Happy Hour Tavern. Their specialties, besides a charming tavern atmosphere, include broasted chicken and homemade cream puffs. Open year-round. Inexpensive.

THE CLUB AT MATHESON GREENS (616) 386-5171. Matheson Road at Swede Road. Warm friendly atmosphere and delicious homemade meals, The Club has everything to create the perfect dining experience. Homemade soups, quiches, and sandwiches. Mouthwatering lunch and dinner specials, and some of the most delicious desserts in the area. Enjoy panoramic views of the Leelanau countryside while you're dining. Inexpensive to moderate.

LELAND

THE BLUEBIRD (616) 256-9081. 102 E. River. Offering great food and warm hospitality since 1927. They have been noted by the *New York*

Times, USA Today, the *Detroit News* and *Free Press,* and the *Chicago Tribune.* The bar is the local watering hole for year-round residents and visitors alike. All have acknowledged this restaurant as a "must stop" for the freshest whitefish, salad bar, grilled steaks and chicken, and seafood and pasta specialties. Heaping baskets of fried smelt, tasty sandwiches, and soup. Winter ethnic feasts change weekly to a different country or culture. A super Sunday brunch with dozens of hot entrées, egg dishes, salads, appetizers, and an array of cakes, pies, and tarts. Moderate to expensive.

THE EARLY BIRD RESTAURANT (616) 256-9656. 101 S. Main (in front of the Bluebird). For hearty breakfasts and light lunches. Delicious hot chocolate and cinnamon rolls. Open year-round. Inexpensive.

SUNSET SQUARE CAFÉ (616) 256-7500. 106 N. Lake (facing the marina). Overlooking the harbor with indoor and outdoor seating, the cafe offers casual foods such as homemade pizza, Coney Island hot dogs, hamburgers, yogurt, and ice cream. Inexpensive.

THE COVE (616) 256-9834. 111 River Street. For atmosphere, you can't beat The Cove, and coupled with wonderful food it's the perfect combination. Dine outdoors next to the waterfall or indoors in a tropical setting. The sunset is fantastic! The Cove is well known for its "Fishtown stew," fresh Lake Michigan whitefish, grilled salmon, prime rib, and authentic key lime pie. Moderate to expensive.

LELAND LODGE (616) 256-9848. 565 E. Pearl. An elegant atmosphere and sophisticated food choices make the Leland Lodge hard to beat. Wonderful appetizers, such as Fishtown dip, terrific whiskey dressing to drizzle over your greens, fresh catch of the day, chicken, and steaks. Relax and enjoy. Occasional entertainment, call ahead. Moderate to expensive.

RIVERSIDE INN (616) 256-9971. 302 E. River. The Riverside Inn has been an established business since 1902. For turn-of-the-century ambience and wonderful gourmet foods, it is a diner's dream. The inn offers a unique blend of fine dining and casual atmosphere, situated overlooking the Leland River. The chef is French trained. The menu changes frequently, and features local produce. Serves gingerbread pancakes, classic eggs Benedict, and fresh baked breads and muffins. Dinner entrees includes smoked pheasant breast with lentil salad, fried ravioli with a gorgonzola cream sauce, and sliced pork tenderloin with a dried cherry sauce. Year-round. Moderate to expensive.

LAKE LEELANAU

DICK'S POUR HOUSE (616) 256-9912. 103 Phillips (downtown Lake Leelanau). Established since 1933, it combines its sportsmen and family tavern-style with true old-time atmosphere. A favorite of locals. Full restaurant and bar menu. Terrific Provemont Charburger. Delicious homemade soups. Chicken, shrimp, and smelt dinners. Inexpensive.

MAPLE CITY

LEELANAU COUNTRY INN (616) 228-5060. 149 E. Harbor Highway (between E. Duck Lake Road—M-204 and Sugar Loaf Resort). *The National Country Inn Publications* has rated the inn "best restaurant in Leelanau County," "best country setting," "best place to go for a drive and have a meal," "best service," and "best Sunday brunch." Seating overlooks a lavish garden area where, while dining, one can glimpse hummingbirds busily gathering nectar. Besides atmosphere, the inn offers pure fresh seafood flown in directly from Boston, and over fifty homemade entrées to choose from. They have the largest selection of Leelanau County vineyard wines. Be seated before 6 p.m. and receive a 15 percent reduction on your food check. Open year-round but you must call ahead because hours and days of operation vary. An absolute must for those who appreciate the best. Moderate to expensive.

SUGARFOOT SALOON (616) 228-6166. A fun and friendly saloon, a favorite of the locals. Authentic Mexican foods, good quality American foods, and a full bar menu. The atmosphere is laid-back and comfortably cozy. Inexpensive.

BENJAMIN'S CAFÉ (616) 228-6692. 8654 Center (downtown Maple City). This is "the little café that could and does." To order a pizza to go or a full sit-down dinner, Benjamin's is a great place and very affordable. Something for every taste from American to Cajun to Mexican. The prime rib special is unbelievable. Open year-round. Inexpensive.

SUGAR LOAF RESORT (616) 228-5461 (ext. 820). Presently the resort features three restaurants.

FOUR SEASONS RESTAURANT. View the slopes and panoramic views of the countryside and Lake Michigan off in the horizon. Elegant atmosphere, coupled with excellent food and well-trained staff make this a special place to dine. Dinner entrées include fresh whitefish, chicken Leelanau, prime rib, seafood linguini, and nightly specials. Shrimp and crab special every Friday and Saturday night. Terrific and extensive Sunday brunch with a knockout dessert bar. Moderate to expensive.

PAR PUB. In the Pro-shop, offering soup, burgers, sandwiches, salads, hot and cold drinks. Relaxing country atmosphere. Inexpensive.

REUBEN TONELLI'S PIZZERIA AND DELI. Inside the main lodge, offering mouth-watering pizza, sandwiches, fresh baked goods, and homemade desserts. Inexpensive to moderate.

CEDAR

CEDAR TAVERN (616) 228-9405. 9037 Kasson. Established in the 1920s. The tavern offers "good ole" bar food, such as delicious burgers, locally made hot dogs, and Polish kielbasa and sauerkraut, excellent homemade chili, and daily meal specials. Highly regarded in this Polish community as a tavern with a friendly, relaxed, atmosphere enjoyed by young and old alike. Open year-round. Inexpensive.

EDDIE G'S ROADHOUSE (616) 228-6266. 8683 County Road 651. A family-style restaurant with a nice country atmosphere. Choices such as chicken, shrimp, steaks, terrific barbecued ribs. Their specialty is pizza. Great breakfasts too. Inexpensive.

GLEN ARBOR

THE HOMESTEAD RESORT (616) 334-5000. M-22 at Westman Road. Presently The Homestead features three restaurants.

THE INN. Dining on the lake. Features modern American cuisine along with the gracious atmosphere of a historic inn. The menu is fresh and ever changing and the views are nothing short of spectacular. Moderate to expensive.

NONNA'S. Dining in the village. Cooks up delicious Italian cuisine served in an informal fieldstone and timber setting. The family-inspired menu offers traditional specialties with a flair. Moderate to expensive.

WHISKER'S. It's the spot for pizza, burgers, and lively entertainment. Inexpensive.

BOONE DOCK'S (616) 334-6444. 5858 Manitou View. The Boone family has done it again—another great restaurant in a rustically elegant atmosphere. Tantalizing Booneburgers, steaks, chicken, and seafood, served in the same great Boone family tradition. Moderate.

GOOD HARBOR GRILL (616) 334-3555. 6584 Western Avenue. Charming, light nautical atmosphere and an innovative menu make this a terrific place to stop. Something different includes Asian pasta, or try grilled chicken served in a Chimichurri marinade. Excellent homemade soups and fresh baked goods.

JOHNNIE SALAMI'S RIVERFRONT PIZZA & SPECIALTIES (616) 334-3876. M-22. Johnnie welcomes you to relax by the riverfront and enjoy a selection from his busy kitchen. He offers pizza, handmade and hand-thrown, thick with blended cheeses and his own special recipe. Gyros, fresh salads, Italian subs, and burgers. Inexpensive.

LE BEAR LANDING (616) 334-4640. 5707 Lake Street. Dining at the Landing offers one of the most panoramic views of Lake Michigan

Dining, Leelanau Style

and the Manitou islands. Moderate to expensive.

THE WESTERN AVENUE GRILL (also known as the Soda Shop). (616) 334-3362. 6410 Western Avenue. Written up in Midwest Living magazine and rightly so. They offer fresh menu ideas to the tired and hungry traveler. A favorite of the locals. Great salads, great Mexican, great Western Avenue favorites including the Glen Arbor Greek, a sandwich you won't forget. Shrimp scampi, steak, crab, pasta, and more. Inexpensive to moderate.

ART'S TAVERN (616) 334-3754 (next to the Standard station on M-22). Since Glen Arbor's early days as a lumber town there has always been a tavern on the corner of M-22 and Lake Street. The place the locals recommend, famous for fresh, homemade foods. Large variety. Homemade sausage, Belgian waffles, soups, chili, and the best burgers. Dinner fare includes whitefish, steak, lasagna, and lots more. Open year-round. Inexpensive to moderate.

EMPIRE

TIFFANY'S (616) 326-5337. 110213 Front Street. A gathering place for the locals, who each have their own mug on display. It's full of that old-fashioned feeling from the early fifties, including the music. Even the cash register (a repository that rings up to a whopping total sale of $3.95) takes you back to 1914. The bar stools are vintage, salvaged from another establishment long ago. They have the distinction of offering the only pasties in Leelanau "direct from da U.P.," and the best in the Grand Traverse area. Fresh donuts and ice cream. Inexpensive.

CLIPPER GALLEY PIZZERIA & DELI (616) 326-5222. 10085 Front Street. The most delicious homemade soups, salads, fresh fruits, sandwiches. The pizza is terrific, with a nice, crispy crust; try a slice of the Hawaiian for a special treat. Fresh baked goods in a glass case brimming full of especially tempting treats. Frozen yogurt. Dine in or carry out. Inexpensive.

EMPIRE VILLAGE INN (616) 326-5101. Corner of M-22 and

Lacore Street. Well-established tavern, featuring tasty appetizers, homemade soups, salads, and excellent homemade pizza. Open year-round. Inexpensive.

JOE'S FRIENDLY TAVERN (616) 326-5506. At Front and Lake streets. Their Friendly burgers for over fifty years have made this a favorite spot. Super breakfasts with homemade pancakes and sausage for starters. Lunch specials, homemade soups, salads, sandwiches. Full dinners with char-grilled steak, seafood, and Mexican entrées. Noted for its homemade streusel pie. Open year-round except December 25. Inexpensive to moderate.

CAFÉ LA RUE (616) 326-5551. M-22, second block past traffic light. Casual dining with a gourmet flair. Soups, salads, and a variety of fresh baked goods and desserts. Breakfast, lunch, and dinner. Lovely indoor atmosphere, or dine outside in a flower-filled courtyard. Occasional entertainment. Moderate.

BURDICKVILLE

GLEN LAKE INN (616) 334-3587. 4566 County Road 616. This inn highlights fine German and American cuisine, fresh fish, pastas, steaks, and seafoods. Old World menu favorites include beef rouladen, Weiner schnitzel, knockwurst and bratwurst, fantastic homemade potato pancakes. New World favorites include roast wild turkey, shrimp scampi, braised pheasant with apples, and flavorful filet mignon. Moderate to expensive.

LA BECASSE (616) 334-3944. Corner of County Roads 616 and 675. Widely acclaimed to be one of the finest French country gourmet restaurants anywhere. The accent is on locally produced foods with frequent creative menu changes. Romantic candlelight atmosphere. Expensive.

6

Gift Shops and Galleries

Unique little shops
Beckon one inside
For memories at home
To daily reside!

    The unique character and beauty of the Leelanau has bred into it some of the finest galleries and shops in the state. The area is a strong magnet for the artistically endowed. Some of the country's most talented artists and artisans live at least part-time in the Leelanau. As for the shops, from antique to contemporary craft, you are sure to find many special treasures to take home along with great memories to bring you back. Shop owners go to special lengths and take great pride in offering their own "look." Many times even the building has a special place in history, having lived in seasons past and continuing to serve for seasons to come.
    Most of the shops are family-owned and run businesses; the proprietors are as helpful as possible. You'll enjoy a laid-back approach to shopping in a fast-paced world.

Gift Shops and Galleries

SUTTONS BAY

If there ever was a town capturing a storybook setting every season of the year, it is Suttons Bay. On the shores of the bay, the town and its people will charm you. Many are reminded of New England, but this is up north with a wonderful identity of its own. Suttons Bay is as old-fashioned as seasons past and as up-to-date as tomorrow.

Suttons Bay post office was established in 1867, and had only an Indian trail between it and Traverse City. Today, it is a short and scenic drive up S. West-Bay Shore Drive (M-22).

Most shops in Suttons Bay are open year-round. Please call ahead when in doubt.

THEATER DISTRICT. In the center of Suttons Bay, east side of St. Joseph.

BAHLE'S (616) 271-3841. 210 St. Joseph Avenue. A store evoking days gone by, established in 1876 by Lars Esten Bahle and run by his offspring. Bahle's has been recognized by the state as a centennial business "Salute to Michigan Business Pioneers." Originally, Bahle's was a general store for the community and housed the post office. Interesting memorabilia are scattered throughout the establishment. Bahle's specializes in fine men's and women's apparel, with a large selection.

THE PAINTED BIRD (616) 271-3050. 216 St. Joseph Avenue. Established since 1987, this elegant gallery is filled with contemporary crafts, unique wearables including custom leather clothing, jewelry, and fine art. The major focus is on local artists but work is on display from around the country. Come in to watch the talented owner as she does custom weavings.

THE ENERDYNE (616) 271-6033. 212 St. Joseph Avenue. The emphasis is on nature and science. You'll note staff member's enthusiasm for merchandise that nurtures an awareness and appreciation of the natural world. Plan to explore The Enerdyne thoroughly. Special

Gift Shops and Galleries

collections and nature/science items on loan are displayed periodically. Don't be surprised by the inclusion of high efficiency wood-burning stoves on the showroom floor. Enerdyne has been a wood stove retailer since 1980. It gets cold up north! Mailing list, catalog, mail order.

BACCHUS & BRIE (800) 729-3180. 220 St. Joseph Avenue. A delightfully upscale gourmet gift shop. Unique sample food tasting bar. Cookbooks and gourmet gift items. Cappucino, Expresso, coffee, and ice cream served. The store offers the largest selection of wines and premium imported beers in the Leelanau peninsula.

THE LIMA BEAN (616) 271-5462. 222 St. Joseph Avenue. Contemporary fashions for women and children.

BAY WEAR (616) 271-4930. 224 St. Joseph Avenue. High-quality T-shirt and sweatshirt designs. Many of the unique designs are created by the owners.

A BIT O' COUNTRY (616) 271-6701. 224 St. Joseph Avenue. In a quiet corner of the Sogee Building. A charming gift shop containing collectibles of all kinds, unique gifts, and cards.

SUTTONS BAY GALLERIES (616) 271-4444. 224 St. Joseph

Leland's Historic Fishtown

Gift Shops and Galleries

Avenue. A fine selection of botanical and nature prints, rare etchings, engravings, limited edition prints from the sixteenth to nineteenth century. Prominent Michigan artists on display.

THE FRONT PORCH (616) 271-6895. 207 St. Joseph Avenue. Established since 1977, a trip into Suttons Bay is not complete without a stop at this well-rounded gift shop. Jams and jellies from the legendary Benjamin Twiggs, gourmet foods, and coffees. A fantastic array of kitchen gadgets, pots, and pans. Recycled card lines. Many accessories for the home as well. Lots of good taste for both the palate and the eye.

ST. JOSEPH AVENUE SHOPS 313 St. Joseph Avenue.

THE BACK FENCE (616) 271-3190. Established since 1979, this shop handles fine merchandise from around the world, including distinctive gifts, greeeting cards, postcards, perfumes, picture frames and photo albums. Also, childen's toys.

EXQUISITE ACQUISITIONS (616) 271-4648. 104 Broadway. Next to the post office. Many handcrafted gift items, local artists' works, and handcrafted baskets. Beautiful photos, framed and matted.

FALCON LEATHER WORKS (616) 271-6490. 103 St. Joseph Avenue. Handcrafted leather and leather accessories designed by the owner, who takes great care and pride in her custom-crafted leather work. Indian art, such as prints and jewelry. Locally made mandalas, beaded earrings, and barrettes. Hats and accessories. A must-stop-to-see high quality shop!

CASE DANIELS (616) 271-3876. 307 St. Joseph Avenue. An exceptional jewelry and gift shop. Silver and gold jewelry, custom work. Beautiful handcrafted leather jewelry, small sculptures, and contemporary paper jewelry.

A BIT OF SUNSHINE & MARILYN'S KITCHEN (616) 271-6449. 105 St. Joseph Avenue. Children's toys, balloons, cards, and gift wrap. Marilyn's Kitchen specializes in homemade chocolate, local honey, maple syrup, and party supplies. Marilyn turns ordinary cake

Gift Shops and Galleries

into a work of art.

KLEIN'S FLOWERS AND GIFTS (616) 271-3751. 209 St. Joseph Avenue. A beautiful floral and gift shop with a full selection of American, European, and tropical flowers. Locally grown dried materials and vines made into beautiful custom pieces. Great ceramic pieces by Michigan artist Gail Yurasek. A large selection of recycled stationery.

THE SILKWORM (616) 271-6305. 311 St. Joseph Avenue. Elegant women's fashions and accessories.

INTER-ARTS STUDIO (616) 271-3891. 326 St. Joseph Avenue. Open since 1965, the store contains an eclectic collection of items from around the world. They handled Mexican glassware for years, long before its popularity today. Interesting rugs and craft items from countries including Russia and Poland. Definitely an interesting place to shop.

GALLERY II (616) 271-4980. 324 St. Joseph Avenue. Art, yarn, and custom framing. Formerly the Art Gallery in Northport.

DANBURY ANTIQUES (616) 271-3211. 305 St. Joseph Avenue. All manner of unexpected antiques. They specialize in English smalls. You'll find a variety of candlesticks, boxes, porcelain dinner services, tea sets, and brasses that the owner has lovingly collected during his frequent trips to England. A must-stop for antique collectors.

LEELANAU ARCHITECTURAL ANTIQUES (616) 271-6821. 301 St. Joseph Avenue. Turn-of-the-century antiques and architectural items, including beveled glass doors, windows, fireplace mantels. Stained glass and other quality turn-of-the-century pieces.

SUTTONS BAY BOOKSTORE (616) 271-3923. 100a Cedar Street. Lots and lots of titles, special Michigan section, postcards, puzzles, top greeting card lines, including Gwen Frostic, and posters by Nell Smith. Extremely helpful service by Mallie Marshall and her staff. Book lovers must stop here.

BRISLING POTTERY (616) 271-3892. 8925 E. Duck Lake Road. On M-204, 1.8 miles west of Suttons Bay. Handcrafted decorative and functional stoneware pottery by Karl and Beverly Sporck. Open daily since 1975. Nature and its varied and beautiful color schemes is their

Gift Shops and Galleries

theme reflecting the beautiful area in which they live and work.

CHERRY COUNTRY SHOPS

Well worth the trip two miles north of town to find these two enterprising businesses.

JOHNNY JOHN'S BOUTIQUE DE BAY (616) 271-4200. 1300 N. Dumas Road. Elegant ladies apparel, jewelry, and gifts uniquely set in a farm-country setting.

BUSHA BRAE'S HERB FARM (616) 271-6284. 2540 N. Setterbo Road. A selection of herbal vinegars, fresh herbs, and specially blended seasonings. Potpourris, books on gardening and herbs, dried flowers, and theme gardens. Victorian afternoon teas featuring herbal teas, breads, cakes, by reservation. The kind of place where you will want to linger.

THE VALLEY

The Valley is a group of rural Leelanau County businesses, who describe their eclectic gathering as "several small business serendiptously situated, more a state of mind than place." The Valley stores are in Bingham Township halfway between Traverse City and Suttons Bay.

BG'S SADDLERY and MORGAN HORSES and STONEBARN PRODUCTS (616) 946-2669. 10210 E. Shady Lane. Equestrian clothing, jewelry, related books, and gift items. Australian outback apparel. The best in tack and horse care products. Handcrafted wood items made by Mr. Hoth.

BELLWETHER HERBS & FLOWERS (616) 271-3004. 10203 E. Shady Lane. Perennial and herb plants, fresh and dried dried herbs and flowers, garden boutique.

BRIGHTHEART POTTERY (616) 271-3052. 5861 S. Elm Valley Road. Susan Brightheart produces a range of esthetically pleasing and functional tableware, and a growing array of porcelain sculpture.

NATURE'S GIFTS (616) 271-6826. 10530 E. Hilltop Road. Nature's gifts are here. Rocks, minerals, and gemstones collected by the Nielsens. Jewelry and sculpture. Items for all ages.

PWEAVINGS PLUS (616) 271-3522. 4519 S. Elm Valley Road. In Mawby's Vineyard. Offering the fruits of Peggy Core's artistic labors. She produces a wide variety of fine arts objects—oil and watercolor paintings, wood-block prints, sculptural pieces of many media, baskets. Handmade jewelry sculptured from handmade paper, and an array of cards. Peggy displays her own style and flair.

MONSTREY'S GENERAL STORE (616) 946-0018. 8332 E. Bingham Road. The proprietor, Dave Monstrey, will greet you. Lots of goodies with the focus on quality and craftsmanship. Berlin Flyers (old-fashioned wooden wagons), Appalachian folk toys, wooden sleds, puzzles, Amish folk dolls, and Amish rocking chairs. Monstrey's offers old-fashioned appeal and service, combined with products with good sense in mind.

LAKE LEELANAU

Lake Leelanau lies between the waters of North and South Lake Leelanau and is halfway between Suttons Bay and Leland on E. Duck Lake Road (M-204).

OUT ON A LIMB (616) 256-7205. 109 Phillips Street (on M-204). This is definitely not a place to miss! Arts and crafts, "Victorian country," home decor, and Southwest and Americana items by area and countrywide artisans. Established since 1984, this has probably become the most successful shop of its kind in the north. Special craft show held each July.

BASKET EXPRESSIONS (616) 256-2222 or (800) 848-3691. 41 N. Eagle Highway (corner of Eagle Highway and E. Duck Lake Road). Specializing in local foods, wines, and gourmet coffees. Gift baskets containing local and gourmet products, shipped anywhere. Wonderful gift selections and a wide variety of books, including chil-

Gift Shops and Galleries

dren's.

THE THUNDERBIRD GIFT SHOP (616) 256-27141. 112 Phillips Street (M-204). Widely known for its wide selection of moccasins. Souvenirs.

OMENA

A small and quaint community midway between Suttons Bay and Northport. In summer you will think you have found paradise in Michigan, this area is exquisite. In winter this area is again very beautiful, with the bark of the white birch trees and the deep snow in stark contrast to the dark blue waters of Omena Bay.

OMENA BAY COUNTRY STORE (616) 386-5850. On M-22 in downtown Omena. An old-fashioned atmosphere greets you as you enter this combination grocery and general store. It has been operating since 1887. Postcards and other necessities.

TAMARACK CRAFTSMAN'S GALLERY (616) 386-5529. On M-22 in downtown Omena. One of the finest galleries in Michigan. Step inside and be transformed into a world full of some of the best talent around. Featuring over a hundred gallery artists and artisans. Contemporary fine and folk art, hand-blown glass, graphics, ceramics, metalworks, fiber works, jewelry, sculpture, and furniture. Open year-round.

CATHY LOOK POTTERY STUDIO (616) 386-7512. 13101 Omena Road. Cathy uses an interesting Japanese process for firing. She has been a potter since 1978.

PESHAWBESTON

Peshawbeston (pronounced p-shaw-bee-town) is an Indian reservation for the Grand Traverse Band of Ottawa and Chippewa Indians.

Gift Shops and Galleries

INDIAN ART STORE (616) 271-3318. On M-22. The Indian Art Store features Woodland Indian art from Indian artists of the Great Lakes region. Select from the finest black ash baskets, quill and birch bark boxes, beadwork, pottery, original oil and acrylic paintings, leather work, greeting cards, and stationery. Some items by the local Indians.

NORTHPORT

A visit to Northport is one you will cherish. Northport, "The Whole Point of the Peninsula," is thirty miles north of Traverse City and eight miles south of the very tip of Michigan's "little finger." On the west shores of Grand Traverse Bay, it exudes authentic, nautically charming atmosphere.

THE SHIPWRECK (616) 386-5878. 209 Boathouse Bay (next to the marina). This historic building was set up in 1949 by noted boat builder Bill Livingston. Many national publications have written about Mr. Livingston, both of his flawlessly crafted boats and his philosophies of life. He was described as a "tough vanishing breed of man, whose very life was his own." Only just recently were the rails used to launch his craft removed to facilitate the remodeling of the new Dame Marina. Since 1970, the building lives on as a gift shop with skippers Fred and Betty Sincock on board, with as much character as the shop itself. The shop offers nautical gifts, authentic shipwreck treasures, lamps, wall sculpture, stationery, sweats, and a large selection of mugs.

NATURE'S GEMS ROCK SHOP (616) 386-7471. Behind The Shipwreck shop. Varied selection of rocks and minerals. Custom cutting and setting. Jewelry, Petoskey stones, and Petoskey polishing kits.

PASSPORT IMPORTS (616) 386-7687. 116 Waukazoo. Crafts gathered from the owner's extensive travels through South and Central America. Some extremely sought-after collectibles are their wall hangings. Jewelry, pottery, tapestries, and toys.

Gift Shops and Galleries

THE COMPASS SPORTS CENTRE (616) 386-5212. 119 Waukazoo. A four-season sports store featuring sports equipment and top brand apparel. **GRANDMA'S TRUNK** (616) 386-5351. Mill Street at Naganoba. Antiques, old bottles, postcards, homemade toys, and country craft.

THE HARBOR SHOP (616) 386-7321. 215 Mill Street. A special shop that reflects the high quality of old European taste and style as well as some purely American nautical pieces. Brass, silver, and copper. Handcrafted jewelry.

THE DEPOT OF HARBOR SPRINGS (616) 386-7221. 104 Nagonaba. Ladies traditional-type clothing with the "east coast" look.

LAND OF AH'S (616) 386-7229. 111 Waukazoo. The specialty here is "wheat weaving from Kansas." Toys, crafts, pottery, and blown glass.

HEATHMAN (616) 386-7006. Understated elegance complements this Victorian antique and finery shop complete with a story of intertwining family history. The building, constructed in 1865, has been home to many different businesses. It has been wonderfully restored, with a charismatic feel the Paffords exude in their shared triumph of a successful restoration. Possibly the most elegant antique shop you will ever encounter.

THE ROSE GARDEN LTD (616) 386-5451. 301 Mill Street. Quite an impressive little gift shop featuring pewter, brass, crystal, native American quill work, jewelry, and furniture pieces. A large selection of carefully selected stationery and greeting cards. Sample some local cherry products to take home.

NORTHPORT SHIRT COMPANY (adjacent to The Rose Garden). Unique Northport and Michigan logo shirts. **COBWEB TREASURES** (616) 386-5532. 393 West Street. "Recycling history" (antiques).

NORTH COUNTRY GARDENS (616) 386-5031. 950 Mill Street. A new location for this extensive gift and garden center with a difference. Beautiful gift and home decor lines carefully and expertly chosen for their excellent taste and appeal. Many items from Central America. Speciality gourmet foods. Jewelry, books, and a large selection of cards and stationery. Fresh flowers and plants. Note their beau-

Gift Shops and Galleries

tiful conservatory.

ARTISAN MEDLEY (616) 7554 201 Mill Street. Forty-some artists are represented here with a fine selection of arts and crafts.

THE BEECH TREE CRAFT GALLERY (616) 386-5200. 202 Waukazoo. "Contemporary crafts in a Victorian cottage beneath a century old copper beach tree." Ceramic and fiber art, wood furniture, jewelry, and handcrafted clothing.

JOPPICH'S BAY STREET GALLERY (616) 386-7428. 109 N. Rose. Since 1980 Joppich's has offered an exciting collection of work by Michigan artists. Over fifty artists are represented with paintings, sculpture, original prints, glass, fine pottery, and wearable art.

VILLAGE ARTS (616) 386-7628. Waukazoo Street. Many of Leelanau artists and craftsmen outshine themselves here. View the paintings by Gene Rantz, jewelry by Judy Mastick, photography by David Brigham, contemporary furniture by Larry Fox, and jewelry design by Martha Eldridge. An interesting selection of local books.

CORNER STORE (616) 386-5761. 101 Mill Street. The oldest business in town. Here everyone, even the locals, get coffee, information, and newspapers. Even an old-fashioned soda fountain completes the scene. There are toys, souvenirs, and drugstore items. The coffee shop in front is open year-round.

SHORELINE (616) 386-5504. 106 Mill Street. Fun clothes for fun people. Surf store without surfboards.

BIRD 'N' HAND (616) 386-7104. 12271 E. Woosley Lake Road (2.5 miles north of town). This is one of the most charming antique shops around and is a definite must-stop for antique lovers. A fantastic array of antique hats, vintage linens, and clothing. Antiques include everything between glassware and furniture.

WOODLAND HERBS (616) 386-5081. 7741 N. Manitou Trail West. A culinary herb shop offering vinegars, rice blends, salt-free seasonings, teas, herb books, herbal beauty baths, wreaths, potpourris, oils, jellies, and chutneys.

VICK-MAURE'S STUDIO (616) 386-7413. M-22 at Camp Haven Road. Hand-painted rock critters. Original stained glass design. Etched glass and glass jewelry.

Gift Shops and Galleries

LELAND

On the shores of Lake Michigan with the Manitou islands as a magnificent backdrop, Leland and historic Fishtown offer many delights to each visitor. In summer the town is busy with people from all parts of the country, basking in the charm. Off season, the town is more navigable for quiet strolling through the colorful shops and streets. Off season, many shops close but even then Leland is pure enchantment.

Most shops are open from mid-May through October, a few through December, and some year-round. During peak season (July and August) most stay open evenings. Off season it is best to call for open hours.

THE GATHERING (616) 256-7779. 407 S. Main Street. "A wee flower shop," fresh flowers, dried arrangements, and plants. Wire and delivery service available. Open year-round.

MAIN STREET GALLERY (616) 256-7787. 307 S. Main Street. Malcolm Chatfield, proprietor, has assembled some of the state's finest artists, some exclusive. His highly knowledgeable eye for art is apparent. Artists include renowned wildlife artist Rod Lawrence (1991 Michigan trout stamp award, 1992 winner of Michigan duck stamp award), Nell Revell Smith, David Grath, Tobin Sprout, and Fred Petroskey. From prints to oils, there is something for everyone. Custom framing also.

WILD BIRDS UNLIMITED (616) 256-2226. 207 N. Main Street. Backyard bird-feeding specialist and complete nature store. Bird feeders, seed, birdbaths, binoculars, books, tapes, clothing, chimes, wildflower seeds, wildlife art, and nature gifts. Trained naturalist staff; morning bird walks in Leelanau County from the store several times a week.

THE MUSEUM STORE (616) 256-7475. 203 E. Cedar Street (the Leelanau Historical Museum, next to the Leland Public Library). If your desire is for something closely linked to the area, look no further than The Museum Store. Original needlework kits, hooking, cross-stitch, and local needlepoint. Many books on both present-day

Gift Shops and Galleries

and historic Leelanau County. Local folk carvings, very nautical, including popular carvings of freighters. Original art and jewelry by Becky Thatcher and Mary Schimpf. A nice selection of black ash basketry. Popular wooden toys. Locally made jams and jellies.

THE LAST STRAW STUDIO (616) 256-9884. 205 Chandler Street. A working studio/shop featuring both original and traditional wheat weaving, batik watercoloring, ceramics, and jewelry.

THE LIVERY BUILDING. Corner of Main and Pearl.

CHERYL'S CLUB COLLECTION (616) 256-0127. A beautiful collection of women's international apparel for those who want style and comfort at reasonable prices. Swimwear, accessories, and unusual jewelry.

LELAND TOY COMPANY (616) 256-7575. This toy store features both American-made and imported toys, including stuffed animals, puppets, kaleidoscopes, books, games, beach toys, and puzzles.

TWISTED CRYSTAL (616) 256-7870. Handcrafted, wire-wrapped jewelry using crystals, natural stones, trader beads, and many other unusual settings. Specializing in dolphin jewelry and one-of-a-kind items.

HARBOR SQUARE 110 Lake Street (near center of town, facing Lake Michigan). The following five shops are in Harbor Square.

PRATTS (616) 256-7366. A sportswear shop featuring sophisticated menswear and gifts.

FLYING COLORS (616) 256-9006. By Leelanau Interiors. A collection of gift items, by local and other American artisans, and imports from around the world. Featuring local prints, posters, photographs. Take the time to browse this one.

RAGAMUFFIN (616) 256-9675. Children's trend-setting clothing and accessories. A must stop for the fussiest buyers. Great end-of-the-

Gift Shops and Galleries

season sale. They carry gifts, books, and toys, too.

ENCORE (616) 256-9670. An outstanding selection of sportswear, swimwear, sweaters, shoes, and accessories.

BARTLINGS (616) 256-9670. A classical selection of women's apparel. Everything from swimwear, sportswear, and dresses. Nice jewelry. A must-stop for the discriminating shopper.

THE FISHHOOK (616) 256-9501. 110 W. River Street. A cozy store fulfilling the boater's and camper's needs, as well as the tourist's. Marine supplies, bait, tackle, fishing licenses, and camping supplies. Large selection of Minnetonka moccasins.

DOUG MURDICK'S FUDGE (616) 256-7241. 110 W. River Street. A trip up north is not complete without taking home some fudge. Fifteen flavors of fudge, peanut and cashew brittle, Benjamin Twiggs cherry products, local honey, and maple syrup. Mail order service available.

AMERICANA COLLECTION OF GIFTS (616) 256-9350. 104 W. River Street. Wonderful antiques and collectibles. Handcrafted gift items by American designers and artisans. A collection of teapots, ceramics, mugs, blown glass, original prints, miniature oils, watercolors, and drawings.

THE OLD LIBRARY (616) 256-7428. 103 W. River Street. Quality antiques and collectibles lovingly on display in a restored mid-1920s building.

RIVER AND MAIN (616) 256-8858. Across from the Harbor Shop. Gifts, gourmet coffees, and food items.

NORTHERN ATTITUDES (616) 256-8859. 104 N. Main Street. A nature shop featuring great items for the outdoors, including birdhouses, wind chimes, furniture, and fountains.

STATICE SEEKERS (616) 256-9120. 112 N. Main Street. Beautiful floral creations hard to resist. A selection of baskets, gift items, and cards.

TIN SOLDIER OF LELAND (616) 256-7530. 113 N. Main Street. The store emphasizes elegant items for home and personal use. Beautiful selections of pottery, decorative pieces, fragrances, stationery, and cookbooks. Something for everyone, with special gifts

Gift Shops and Galleries

not just found "anywhere."
LELAND HARBOR HOUSE (616) 256-7530. 109 N. Main Street. Gifts, jewelry, and a terrific selection of sportswear, souvenir sweats, and T-shirts, for children and adults. Beach towels.
LEELANAU BOOKS (616) 256-7111. 109 N. Main Street. Prudence Mead adds her charm and great knowledge to her full-service bookstore, specializing in local authors, Michigan books, and a terrific children's section. A fine selection of old and rare books.
FOLLOWING SEA (616) 256-7179. 101 N. Main Street. Creative designs in jewelry, wind chimes, T-shirts, wood marquetry, executive gifts, and Black Hills Gold.
FROM THE HEART (616) 256-CARD. 107 N. Main Street. Mostly greeting cards.
MOLLY'S (616) 256-7540. 105 N. Main Street. Charming shop specializing in ladies sportswear and hand-knit sweaters. Locally made jewelry. Very helpful staff and service.

LELAND COURTYARD 104 N. Main Street. The following six shops are in Leland Courtyard.

KIMS KARGO (616) 256-7106. An elegant little shop filled with special sweaters and unusual accessories.
JEANETTE'S PETITE FASHIONS (616) 256-9320. Petite fashions and accessories. Purchases mailed home for your convenience. Beautiful selections.
TAMPICO IMPORT (616) 256-7747. This colorful shop carries unique items that the owner has found on her many travels. Mexican folk art, glassware, pottery, Navajo rugs, many of which are collectible to the highest degree. Northern Michigan's "largest selection" of sterling silver jewelry, Navajo, Zuni, Mexican, and contemporary pieces.
MICHIGAN PEDDLER (616) 256-7685 or (800) 729-3180. Pride and a special kind of love for Michigan gave birth to this unique shop. The owners have taken special efforts to bring their customers wonderful items from artists and artisans across our very talented state.

Gift Shops and Galleries

Books, perpetual wooden calendars, bird feeders, wind chimes, and more. The largest selection of wines in all of northern Michigan. Jams, jellies, and condiments made locally.

MANITOU OUTFITTERS (616) 256-7231. Leelanau County's headquarters for classic outdoor wear featuring top brands of clothing and boots. Gift items, including buck knives to beach chairs. This sophisticated store takes great pride in personal service for its discriminating shoppers.

INLAND PASSAGE (616) 256-9900 or (800) 626-5432. Unique selection of handcrafted items and functional art reflecting the sights and sounds of northern Michigan. Call for free catalog.

FISHTOWN.

At the mouth of Carp River and Lake Michigan. The following ten shops are in Fishtown.

LEELANAU LEATHER (616) 256-9017. At the same location since 1972, this shop has a wide selection. Natural fiber clothing, ethnic jewelry, animal puppets. Leather goods featuring an exclusive line of bags and purses. Largest selection of hats in the area.

THE NET SHED (616) 256-7448. A collection of contemporary men's and boys' swim, resort, and casual wear.

THE ICE HOUSE: CARP RIVER TRADING (616) 256-9691. The shop has the distinction of being the only remaining icehouse that served the fishing industry at the beginning of the century. It is home to a retail, wholesale, and mail order establishment, and has wonderfully delicious items to tempt your taste buds. Preserves, toppings, condiments, and candy. Their barbecue sauce is fantastic. Special, attractive gift boxes featuring renowned wildlife artist Rod Lawrence. Carp River T-shirts designed by Rod Lawrence, coffees, and more.

LAUGHING FISH (616) 256-8878. The fun stuff shop, great beach things, inflatables, kites, T-shirts, and more. Bicycle rentals by half day, daily or weekly.

Gift Shops and Galleries

FISHTOWN DESIGNS (616) 256-9810. Located under the Ice House. Diverse collection of fun and fishy jewelry, and gift pieces to take home to remind you of this colorful area. A commitment to sterling and stone as well as works from other times and other lands.

LELAND BEACH COMPANY (616) 256-7600. Shoes for the boaters and those who wish they were.

PORT HOLE (616) 256-9061. Fun gifts for everyone are stowed aboard this delightful gift shop. It's guaranteed you will find something to make you laugh here. Cards, mugs, T-shirts, stickers, gift wrap, and Leland ceramic magnets. Manitou Island Transit tickets are available here.

LIMITED, LTD. (616) 256-9787. Clothing, jewelry, nice selection of children's toy items, beach towels, and 14K gold.

REFLECTIONS (616) 256-7820. Many beautiful items "reflecting" the Leelanau area. Art, large selection of environmental tapes, gift items accenting nature, beautiful prints, and watercolors.

FISHTOWN CANDY COMPANY (616) 256-9276. Leland's largest selection of candy. Choose by the piece or by the pound.

GLEN ARBOR

Glen Arbor is a blend of history and hospitality. Many of its shops and accommodations of today are at sites settled by the pioneers of Leelanau. The Homestead resort is at the mouth of the Crystal River, where John LaRue established the first permanent white residence on the Leelanau mainland in 1847. Today's artists in the Lake Street Studios identify with John C. Fisher, who arrived in 1854 and owned a thousand acres on the north side of Glen Lake. Sylvan Inn and the bookseller and artists in the Lake Isle Shops in Glen Arbor West are on land settled in 1856 by Fisher's friend, William Walker.

TOTEM SHOP (616) 334-3533. 6521 Western Avenue. This shop was established in 1938 and was originally called The Glen Arbor

Gift Shops and Galleries

Gift Shop. Its present owners have kept with the tradition of the truly up north atmosphere with its warm knotty pine paneling. Walk back in time when browsing this one. They offer moccasins, Indian dolls and toys, Doug Murdick's fudge, American Spoon Foods, stationery, books, camera supplies, and sundries.

THE COTTONSEED (next to The Totem Shop). (616) 334-6254. Charming ladies apparel shop specializing in sportswear, including lots of swimsuits.

PETOSKEY PETE'S (616) 334-3505. 6548 Western Avenue. A nice selection of silk-screened clothing and summer collectibles. Mountain bike rentals.

WILDFLOWERS (616) 334-3232. 6127 Manitou Trail. The Leelanau has many gift shops and this is one of the best. Wildflowers carries gifts and accessories for the home charmingly displayed in an antique setting. Take the time to browse, inside and outside. There is an extensive selection of perennials and wildflowers as well as statuaries, wind chimes, and other garden art in the lovely woodland gardens.

DICKINSON GALLERY (616) 334-4183 or 4835. 7545 W. Glennere. (M-22, half mile west of Glen Lake Narrows). A gallery steeped in the history of the Sleeping Bear Dunes area. Contemporary works and realistic hand-colored photographs by Grace Dickinson Johnson. Dunescape and other photos by Al Millstein. Historical photographs by Fred Dickinson, such as dune car rides from the 1950s, Leland Fishtown photos from the 1930s to present, maps and postcards of the area. Established since 1938. Fred and Julia printed the Leelanau Enterprise in the gallery during the years 1943 through 1948.

GLEN ARBOR CITY LIMITS (616) 334-4424. 6610 Western Avenue (M-109). Established in 1987, this shop is open year-round. The gallery offers a rich mixture of American handcrafts and fine art. Emphasis is on the romantic pioneer and rustic traditions as well as on the cultural heritage of the American Indians. Find items such as twig furniture, birch bark containers and frames, cowboy memorabilia, vintage circus chairs, and artwear. The artists represented are nationally

Gift Shops and Galleries

and internationally acclaimed.

LEELANAU INTERIORS (616) 334-4754. 6654 Western Avenue (M-109). Interior design experts and much more. Specializes in hand-crafted, hand-painted furniture, fabulous rugs, accessories, linen, jewelry, and many more irresistible items.

BECKY THATCHER DESIGNS (616) 334-3826. 5795 Lake Street. More than just a design studio. Becky Thatcher captures the very essence of northern Michigan's beauty, legends, and lore with her jewelry. Each fall Becky and staff walk the beaches of Sleeping Bear Bay picking up favorite rocks, granite, quartz, jasper, and the hard-to-find Petoskeys. Over the winter, they fashion the beach rocks into beads and cabs, mounting them in silver and gold. Thus their customers can take home a part of Sleeping Bear Bay to rekindle fond memories of sunsets, campfires, and quiet walks along the beach. Of special note is Becky's "legend" necklaces. Stop in and find out why.

VILLAGE SAMPLER SHOPS. 5915-5919 S. Glen Lake Road (M-22).

TINY TREASURES (616) 334-3874. A full-service gift shop, featuring "gifts from the heart." A large assortment of gifts, books, cards, and stationery for all ages. Great assortment of watercolors by local artists. Fine collectibles, easy-listening music, and home accessories.

THE BLACK SWAN (616) 334-4045. "Resortwear with panache," a selection of casual clothing, sportswear, distinctive jewelry and accessories. Color and wardrobe consultation available.

LAKE ISLE SHOPS 6632 N. M-109. Attractive and inviting garden seating surrounded by the following three shops.

KEN SCOTT PHOTOGRAPHY (616) 334-6101. Talented and well-known photographer; has had photo books published, *Michigan's Leelanau County* and *Still, M!ch!gan.* Plan on taking some time to glean

Gift Shops and Galleries

the many photos of northern Michigan on display in his gallery. Beautiful three-dimensional photo collages. Stunning photos of the northern lights spectacle that occurred November 8, 1991, featured in the *Detroit News*. Ken Scott offers a great way to take home a part of Leelanau as well as other northern destinations.

RUTH CONKLIN STUDIO (616) 334-3880. A very talented artist, well-noted for her hand-pulled block prints using nature and the Sleeping Bear Dunes as inspiration for her lovely prints. The studio has a nice selection of pottery, jewelry, handwovens, handcrafted wearables and baskets. Lots of great fishy stuff and items for dog and cat lovers.

THE COTTAGE BOOK SHOP (616) 334-4223. You will be met by a warm smile as proprietor Mollie Weeks greets you. The shop is comfortable and warm and invites one to stay and sit for a while. Current fiction, nonfiction, teen and children's, Michigan history, native American, Great Lakes, local and regional books, as well as antique and collectible books. A great place for a good book to take to the beach or a treasure for your home collection.

THE ARBOR LIGHT (616) 334-3165. 5972 Lake Street. Listed as a historical site, the building was built in 1892 and still carries the feelings of yesteryear. The store has country fabrics galore, rugs, baskets, craft books, pewter, and lots more. A fine selection of hanging and bedding plants.

GLEN LAKE ARTIST GALLERY (616) 334-4603. (adjacent to the Arbor Lite on Lake Street). A talented group of local artists has assembled a very fine gallery here of paintings, photography, jewelry, wearables, glass, ceramics, fibers, wood, and more. A must-stop in Glen Arbor.

LAKE STREET STUDIOS (616) 334-6112. 6023 Lake Street. Working/Teaching studio under the auspices of the Glen Arbor Art Association, Inc. Offering classes and workshops in pottery, weaving, painting, and jewelry for children and adults. Classes held from June through August. For free brochure write P.O. Box 305, Glen Arbor, MI 49636.

Gift Shops and Galleries

THE SPORTSMAN SHOP (616) 334-3872. On M-22. Men and women's sporting goods with top brands.

ANANDA BRICKER FOREST FLOWER STUDIO (616) 334-4603. 6847 S. Dune Highway M-109 (on Glen Lake across from the Sand Dune Climb). A beautiful gallery, not to miss. Porcelain and copper wildflower sculpture, watercolor paintings, and jewelry.

THE DUNE STAND (616) 334-3853. At the foot of the climb up the Sleeping Bear Dunes. The shop offers gifts, toys and souvenirs, and a large selection of books on the area.

THE VILLAGE SHOPS AT THE HOMESTEAD (616) 334-5000.

M-22 at Westman Road. Discover the Village Shops, a quaint gathering of small shops in a premier "Freshwater Resort." Seasonal changes in shops bring lots of fresh places to explore. Call The Homestead for current shopping information. Whether you are staying at the Homestead or elsewhere, this is a must-stop for shoppers.

EMPIRE

Sitting next to the Sleeping Bear Dunes, Empire is headquarters for The Sleeping Bear Dunes National Lakeshore. Downtown Empire is tucked in a bit off the main highway, but it's worth it to get off the beaten track and explore the commercial district. Be sure to visit the Robert Manning Memorial Lighthouse, dedicated in 1991, at the municipal beach in Empire, which gives off it's protective beam to boater's coming in after dusk. Mr. Manning was an avid fisherman who lived in Empire all his life who really felt this light was needed. The family decided to build the light to safely guide the way as a tribute to a man deeply loved and missed.

LEELANAU HISTORICAL MUSEUM (616) 326-5568. On M-22 (Just north of the M-72 intersection). A place not to miss if you desire to learn more of the history of the area. The museum gift shop has many books, both of local and historical nature. The museum also publish their

79

Gift Shops and Galleries

own books by local residents, and is known as the Empire Heritage Group. There is also a large selection of reproduction toys for that special someone on your list.

THE SLEEPING BEAR STORE (616) 326-5433. 11690 M-22 (north of the blinker light on M-22). "Souvenirs of the Sleeping Bear to eat and wear." Clothing, beach accessories, and local goodies.

EMPIRE CLIPPER TRADING COMPANY (616) 326-5518. 10085 Front Street. All kinds of goodies are gathered here where even the shop owner is a colorful character. Gourmet section filled with fresh coffee beans, jams and jellies, spices, and herbal teas. Cute little gift baskets.

THE SECRET GARDEN (616) 326-5428. 10206 Front Street. Featuring the works of Midwestern artists and craftsmen. Photography, watercolors, wood block prints, pottery, jewelry, fiber arts, and children's toys are part of their selection.

LEAH-ARTWEAR (616) 326-5426. 10228 Front Street. Selection of hand-painted wearables, including dresses, coats, denim jackets, sweatshirts, and T's. Jewelry by local artists.

BLUE HERON GALLERY AND SCHOOL (616) 326-5505. 10097 Front Street. An art gallery in summer and a creative school for grades 1-4 in the fall.

THE SHOREBIRDS (616) 334-4690. 8690 County Road 616. Run by internationally renowned wildlife carver Russ Van Houzen; a gallery for all nature lovers. Duck decoys, songbirds, and fish. Commission a carving of your favorite species.

BOARD & BASKET (616) 326-5461. 11572 LaCore. Has many one-of-a-kind gifts made by local artisans plus quality artwork, baskets, brass, dolls from around the world. Local maple syrup and cherry products.

THE COUNTRY SHOP. On M-72 (six miles east of Empire). A country store, in a huge updated barn, with a great selection. Over a hundred local artisans display their crafts, soft sculpture, wood products, ceramics, clothing, and home accessories. A room full of teacher's supplies. Antiques. You will be impressed with the quality and the quantity found here.

Gift Shops and Galleries

CEDAR

Leelanau's "Polish Town." Even the grocery stores are interesting and offer some special delights such as Pleva's homemade cherry sausage and the highly acclaimed low-fat beef and cherry hamburger mixture. Check it out.

MAPLE CITY

Near the heart of the county; has "Mayberry" style and a definite "laid back" atmosphere.
MICHIGAN TRADERS, LTD. (616) 228-7459. 497 E. Harbor Highway (M-22, eight miles south of Leland). If she doesn't yet have it, Jill Baxter will soon be getting it; this shop is growing by leaps and bounds. Michigan and nature books, stationery, postcards, hand-loomed rugs, Michigan copper, pottery, decoys, jewelry, Michigan gourmet foods and wines. And more.
SVOBODA POTTERY (616) 228-6394. 6758 S. Maple City Highway. Talented potter offering high-fired porcelain and stoneware pottery. Her Czechoslovakian name, meaning "freedom," is reflected in her beautiful pieces. Hours vary; please call ahead.
LEELANAU TRADING COMPANY (616) 228-6575. 13030 S. Coleman Road. Twelve miles west of Traverse City on M-72. A rustically designed building seemingly stuck in the middle of nowhere. Ted Gilmer's natural motif includes handmade cotton and wool sweaters, hats, mittens, and blankets. Custom leather backpacks and luggage. Handcrafted, cedar stripped, wooden canoes and small row boats. Factory outlet for "scuppers" hand-woven boat shoes. This is worth the drive.

7

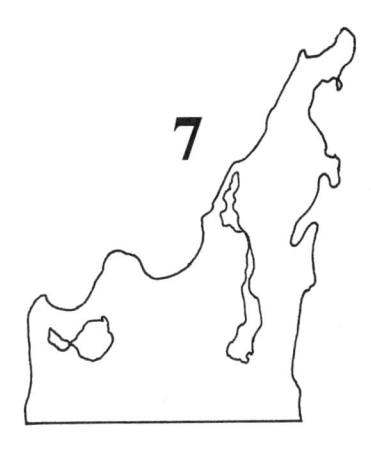

Fruit of the Leelanau

Spring flows sweetly
To the Leelanau
Blessing her fruit
Veins running so deeply.

    Leelanau County is ideally situated at the forty-fifth parallel, moderately elevated with warm sandy loam and glacial moraines, the deposits of ridges and rock heaps, and the right climate tempered by the westerly winds off Lake Michigan. These favorable conditions, like those in France, make it ideal for the growing of fruit. The first white settlers, in the early nineteenth century, saw its potential for fruit growing. So began what has become one of the prime fruit-growing counties in the nation.

CHERRIES

By the mid-nineteenth century both Rev. George Smith and Rev. Peter Doughtery noted success in their orchards, which included cherries. Over the next forty years most pioneer farmers included a few cherry tree in their orchards. Surplus crops were sold to local stores or in Traverse City and shipped by boat to commission houses in Chicago and Milwaukee.

The first commercial orchards were planted in the 1880s. Through the years the Leelanau has boasted some of the largest cherry orchards in the United States. "Cherry Home," which stretched across the peninsula near Northport, was at one time the largest cherry orchard in the world.

When cherries are ripe, they must be harvested immediately and processed quickly. Cherries were laboriously pitted by hand until late 1910 when the Dunkley pitting machine simplified the procedure. The cherry industry got a big boost when grower Birney Morgan built the first canning company in 1912. Other methods of preservation, freezing, and brining were added in the 1920s.

From the 1890s through the early 1960s, all cherries were handpicked. The first picking crews were the growers' families, and included the Ottawa and Chippewa. By the late 1920s the crops became to large for just the local help to manage. Many Leelanau residents remember men described as "hoboes" arriving on "Old Maud," the engine on the Traverse City to Northport line, to pick the cherries. During the depression these men were joined by families from both Lower Michigan and the southern states, who lived in tents during the short cherry-picking season. During World War II all the folks at home, along with POWs, college students, vocational school inmates, girls at summer camp, housewives, children—anyone who was fit—were recruited. After the war distinct patterns of migration evolved. Crews of black men came with a boss, who transported and fed them. Mexican and Afro American families came to pick. On North Manitou Island crews of Mexicans and Jamaicans were brought on to work.

Presently there are over eleven thousand acres of cherry orchards, dynamic and vital to the Leelanau. The orchards offer scenic beauty and a rural serenity for residents and visitors alike to savor. These orchards produce 25 percent of the Michigan cherry crop, quite a share!

Many of these lovely orchards are being sold off to become platted for subdivisions, especially so for water-view properties. This real estate is becoming much in demand and can command high prices, making it attractive to the often strapped farmer.

Fruit of the Leelanau

CHERRY BLOSSOM TIME

As the sun begins to gently warm the hills of the Leelanua in April and May, the dormant buds of the cherry trees begin to develop. Blossom time is critical for the delicate blossoms. Most of the cherry blossom is made up of water, when the temperature falls below 32^0 F, the fragile blooms may freeze and be damaged.

As a rule, depending on weather conditions, sweet cherries bloom about the first part of May. Tart cherries bloom about mid-May. During full bloom, pollination of the cherry blossoms by bees is critical. Contrary to popular opinion, cherry blossoms have little fragrance, depending on the amount of nectar produced. But the loveliness of orchards in blossom make up for that fact.

PEACHES, PLUMS, PEARS, AND APPLES

Peaches, pears, and plums have been grown in this county since 1850. The first fruit farmer was Rev. George Smith, who set out twenty peach trees. At that time in New Mission (Omena) peaches were as great a marvel as apples. States the Leelanau Enterprise of September 23, 1880: "About 500 bushels of apples were shipped on the Fountain City to Chicago."

About 150 species of historical apples are grown in Leelanau. By 1862, Rev. Smith had 150 apple trees, and apples of this planting are still being harvested.

FARM MARKETS

Many small roadside farm stands are scattered about the hills and valleys of Leelanau County. Listed below are a few favorites.

Fruit of the Leelanau

KILCHERMAN'S (616) 386-5637. 11573 N. Kilcherman Road. Northport, MI 49670. Over 175 varieties of apples produced and sold. Gift baskets shipped throughout the country. Mr. Kilcherman is acclaimed for his knowledge about apple species, especially in relation to their historical significance and tracings to present strains.

GALLAGHER'S FARM MARKET (616) 947-1689. 7237 M-72 West, Traverse City, MI 49684. Farm market, fresh baked goods, and local gift items. A great place to stop on your way from Traverse City to the dunes.

FLYING SCOTT'S FARM (616) 271-3871. 430 Wahl Road, Suttons Bay, MI 49682. Farm market with prime quality sweet cherries for the fresh market; also a small peach orchard.

GOOD HARBOR FRUIT FARM (616) 256-7165. 34 North Manitou Trail West (M-22), Lake Leelanau, MI 49653. Adjacent to Good Harbor Vineyards. Home-grown fruits and vegetables, bakery, deli, and specialty foods, including homemade jams, jellies, and relish. Local maple syrup.

MAPLE SYRUP

It is believed that the Woodland Indians discovered maple syrup centuries ago. Before copper kettles became available, the Indians would boil down maple syrup by placing hot stones in a bark-lined trough. Much later, the Indians at New Mission (Omena) made a business of sugar making in the spring. When the temperature began to rise and the snow was beginning to melt, they erected their camps in the maple forests and began to tap the trees.

The Indians made several products from the sap. They called the syrup "se- wa-ga-ma-da." The delicious wax was known as "peg-a-wa-da." The sugar product was named "siz-a-bah-qua." Often they would pulverize the sugar and pack it into birch bark boxes called "mococks." These boxes had a capacity of 80 to 100 pounds. This was a merry time for the Indians and was anticipated for many months.

Fruit of the Leelanau

The trees are still being tapped. Modern sophisticated methods bring us just as tasty a syrup as was enjoyed by the first Leelanau residents. You can visit the Michigan Centennial Farm, Sugar Shack, to enjoy nature's delicious gift.

SUGAR SHACK (616) 228-5835. 3493 W. Baatz Road, Maple City, MI 49664. "Delicious gifts from nature" highlight the Sugar Shack. This is a seventh generation Michigan Centennial Farm. Stop in the springtime to see where the sap is collected by their modern tubing system from over nine thousand sugar maples, on their two hundred-acre "bush." After the sap is pumped to the Sugar Shack, it is boiled down to syrup. This is Michigan's largest and most efficient syrup producer.

The maple syrup is available in a variety of sizes and containers. They have honey, cherry jam, and exclusive Sugar Shack gift boxes. Mail orders also.

GRAPES TO WINE

What better way to bring to life the complicated and seasonally dependent task of wine making than to ask a wine maker. Bill Skolnic, general manager and wine maker for Leelanau Wine Cellars, takes us through a wine-making season:

> Autumn, specifically mid-September to the end of October, is a nerve-racking time. I am a wine maker, and once a year I have a chance to make the best wine possible from that year's vintage.
>
> I depend on the Leelanau, on the soil, the weather, and, most of all, the water.
>
> The 1989 vintage was particularly memorable. It started out as a nightmare. The weather became erratic as it usually does after Labor Day. Temperatures fluctuated wildly from highs in the sixties during the day to the mid-thirties at night. High winds and torrential downpours collaborated with the temperature to take that year's chance for me—the chance to make a great wine.

I became more dependent on the Leelanau as the weather worsened. I prayed to no one in particular to allow the soil to quickly drink the rain, keeping the water from the roots. If the roots absorbed the water, the grapes would swell, diminishing their character. I prayed that the deep water of Grand Traverse Bay and Lake Michigan would fight the cold fronts attacking mercilessly each night. Give up your heat, Your Majesty, moderate the climate, help the grapes survive.

As September's weeks passed and October was nearing, my thoughts turned to Indian Summer. The Leelanau would provide it, I was sure. The weather will moderate, the grapes will bask in a week or two more of sunshine, and soon we will drink the fruit of the vine.

One more front was forecast, then one very bad killer front—lows in twenties two days away. Devastation on the way, we raced to the vineyard and picked at a furious pace. We were winning. One by one, the vines gave up the fruit. First Pinot Noir, the chardonnay, then Vignoles, and the Reisling.

The front hit early the next morning with the Reisling still on the vine. The grapes were literally frozen solid; the leaves had turned from a dark green to light brown. As the front moved through, it blew the leaves right off their vines, leaving the canes naked, the grapes exposed. A thick coat of frost insulated the frozen berries.

We harvested the Reisling that morning, the last grapes to come out of the vineyard. Had the Leelanau failed us, or had it helped us fight to the bitter cold end to harvest the best grapes possible? We would know the answer in the spring.

Meanwhile, we pressed the frozen Reisling grapes; thousands of tiny little ice balls reluctantly gave up their sweet nectar. The juice was rich and sweet because the sugar did not freeze. We had made ice wine and it has won three different gold medals.

The Leelanau did not let us down; she protected us and our crop to the bitter end.

Michigan ranks fourth in the United States in grape growing and fifth in wine production, at present. The federal government has recognized four viticultural or grape-growing regions in the state: Old Mission Peninsula, Lake Michigan Shore, Fennville, and the Leelanau peninsula. Although Michigan winemaking dates to the 1880s, the

Fruit of the Leelanau

early wines were sweet and syrupy, made from concord grapes. Table wine began in the modern sense in the early 1960s in the southwest part of the state. The industry spread its way north in the 1970s along the shores of Lake Michigan through the state's fruit belt, which runs to Grand Traverse Bay. The 1980s saw the continued expansion of Michigan's wine industry. The state developed the Grape and Wine Council, allocating a substantial part of the tax paid by the industry to promote research and marketing.

Northwest Michigan, noted more for harsh, snowy winters than its wines, consistently produces some of the nation's best wines. Even California wine producers acclaim Leelanau's success. That wine-quality grapes can even survive, let alone thrive in northern Michigan's climate can be traced over a hundred years ago to Europe. In the 1880s, Phylloxera plant lice, which attacks grapevine roots, nearly wiped out the vineyards of France. Scientists were prompted to graft French *Vitus Vinifera* with hardy American root stock resulting in a vine that could stand up to adversity. The "French Hybrid" was born; advancements were continually made to the point that the plants could live in the north.

The growth of the American wine industry is, however, equated with the expansion of the California vineyards. That growth was stimulated by massive plantings of the *Vitus Vinifera,* table wine grapes, namely chardonnay, Pinot Noir, cabernet sauvignon, and others brought to this country from the great vineyards of France.

In the east and Midwest, concern existed that the *Vitus Vinifera* grapes could not withstand the heavy winters. Hardier and more prolific French hybrid varieties were planted for table wine development. These varieties enabled the wineries in these regions to transform from sweet wine producers to producers of dry table wines. However, these varieties did not have the name recognition that the *Vitus Vinifera* did.

By the late 1970s these growers and producers realized that this reliance on French hybrid grapes could impair their competitiveness, and began experimenting with Vitus Vinifera. By the late 1980s chardonnays, Reislings, and other well-known wines from *Vitus*

Vinifera were competing from the East and Midwest nationally with California and the world.

The Leelanau region's secret to its success is the microclimate created by the moderating effects of Lake Michigan, Lake Leelanau, and Grand Traverse Bay. The lakes store up the summer heat, which results in an extended autumn. This same heat warms the Arctic blasts of winter, so the area does not receive the sudden temperature plunges that can be fatal to tender grape varieties. The deep winter snows protect the grapevines' root systems from harsh freeze- thaw patterns. Moderate summer temperatures result in a slow-ripening process and later harvest. Hot weather saps grapes and other fruits of their acids; cooler temperatures make for a fruitier, more distinctive tasting grape and better wines. It is an area of low relative humidity, which helps prevent fungus diseases.

The forty-fifth parallel crosses through the midsection of the Leelanau, as it does though the province of Bordeaux, France. Therefore it became logical that the region's microclimate would attract local fruit growers to the growing of grapes. Catching sight of these well-tended vineyards is a very beautiful sight, making one think somehow he is in those of France.

There are four primary vineyards in the Leelanau; one of these, Leelanau Wine Cellars, is the second largest in the state. Good Harbor Vineyards, L. Mawby Vineyards, and Boskydel are the other three. Other vineyards are being planned in this nouveau wine region. Great attention has been given to the Leelanau peninsula by wineries the world over. Surely this area will continue to build on its growth and success in companionship with the best of wineries anywhere.

LEELANAU WINE CELLARS (616) 386-5201. 12693 E. Tatch Road, Omena, MI 49674. "At the top of the hill" in Omena, a small and very quaint village overlooking Grand Traverse Bay, twenty-two miles north of Traverse City. The winery is on six scenic acres of land. The buildings were converted from their historical cherry farm use.

Leelanau Wine Cellars produces premium red and white varietal table wines and other blended wines. To promote its regionalism it also promotes natural fruit wines and other local products.

Thirty-five acres are currently planted; there are plans to expand to sixty acres in the near future. Result: the production of seventeen thousand cases of wine bottled in 1991, and a future goal of thirty-five thousand cases being produced annually. Open year-round for wine tasting and tours.

GOOD HARBOR VINEYARDS (616) 256-7165. 34 N. Manitou Trail West (M-22). Three miles south of Leland, this is well worth a stop both for its winery and the farm market next door.

Founded in 1980, Good Harbor Vineyards is the second largest winery in the Leelanau. It retains its small family-owned aura nicely. They began planting wine grapes in the 1970s and have focused on making the best possible wine.

This focus is evident in the meticulous way they take care of their vineyard and their wine cellar. The vineyards are carefully hand-pruned, hand- tied, and hand-harvested. The wines are handled only minimally. The only processing techniques used are those that don't alter the inherent fruit character of the wine.

Some of the wines they produce are Trillium, a semidry blend, the essence of northern Michigan wines, with an intense fruity aroma, and a chardonnay, fermented in white oak, a satisfying blend of fruit and oak. More like European chardonnays than chardonnays on the West Coast.

They have been growers of sweet and tart cherries for many years. Their cherry wine is made with the same devotion to quality that their grape wine receives. This wine is a blend of dark English Morello cherries and light juiced Montmerency cherries with just a touch of cherry juice just before bottling to give it some sweetness.

Tours and tastings are offered seven days a week, May 25 through November 1. In the winter, they are open on occasional Saturdays; please call ahead for specifics.

L. MAYBY VINEYARDS (616) 271-3522. 4561 E. Elm Valley Road, Suttons Bay, MI 49682. The vineyards and the winery are tucked into a beautiful thirty-two acre parcel of rolling hills in Suttons Bay. Larry Mayby's personal goal has always been to produce the finest wines possible, with strict attention to the vineyards, the cellar, and the winegrower's esthetic. His view is that "wines are living things raised with care to give voice to our joie de vivre."

First vines were planted in the spring of 1973. Estate grown and bottled Leelanau peninsula table wines have been produced since the first crush in 1978. Principally, they make white table wines, but their is an increase in sparkling wines each year. Production of red and rosé wines is limited.

Current annual production is twenty-four hundred cases; the ultimate goal is three thousand cases. The vineyards comprise twelve acres of land; there are plans to add another four to six acres over the next few years.

The hours are limited to enable the winery to welcome visitors, yet leave time to the chores of a winegrower. The winery is open to the public from May 1 through October 31 on Thursday, Friday, and Saturday from 1 p.m. to 6 p.m. Visits at other hours may be arranged by appointment.

BOSKYDEL VINEYARD (616) 256-7272. 7501 E. Otto Road, Lake Leelanau, MI 49653. Boskydel Vineyards has an idyllic setting: under a grove of pines overlooking 25 acres of planted vineyards and lovely South Lake Leelanau. Boskydel has the distinction of being the first bonded wine cellar in the Leelanau.

This is a "family enterprise"; the proprietor, his wife, and his sons began testing hybrid grapes in 1965. They truly believed that the hills along Lake Leelanau would afford them success in this endeavor. Their vineyards reflect their intense commitment to producing fine wines. Current production ranges between six to twelve thousand gallons per year.

Their grapes are French-American hybrids with the disease resistance of American roots. The wines that have derived from these marriages have a definite European character and range from good to excellent. Discover wines that include Vignoles, Seyval Blanc, and DeChaunac, each with its own varietal and blend. Distinctive in both body and bouquet, fruity when young and mellow when aged.

The winery is open year-round from 1 p.m. to 6 p.m. daily.

8

Seasons of the Maritime

*Pounded by mighty waves, turning gentle
At a whisper, from some hidden place on high.
Emerald isles off her horizon,
Which countless men have sailed by.*

    A visit to the Leelanau is not complete without a consideration of the rich maritime history, so much a part of her legacy.
    Navigating the waters of the Great Lakes has been at times hazardous. In the past, courageous men volunteered their efforts in early rescue attempts. Many times their training and equipment were inadequate. During the post-Civil War period, shipping increased, creating the need for a lifesaving organization to care for the sailors at sea. The United States life-Saving Service was created in 1871 and existed until 1915, when the present-day Coast Guard was established. On the Great Lakes, sailing vessels and steamers were many, carrying cargoes of lumber from the great forests, grain from the farmland, iron ore from the earth, and other products. During the severe winter

of 1870-1871, 214 people lost their lives in shipwrecks on the Great Lakes. The U. S. Coast Guard's Lighthouse Automation Program (LAMP) began in 1968 and was completed in 1990. This ended more than a hundred years of manned lighthouse operation. Following is a short recap of the part the Leelanau has played in the seasons of the maritime, today preserved for us by the efforts of many people.

SLEEPING BEAR POINT COAST GUARD MARITIME MUSEUM.

The Sleeping Bear Point lifesaving station is listed on the National Register of Historic Places. This museum takes one back to seasons long ago when valiant men risked their lives to help the sailors who dedicated themselves to the Great Lakes. Let the past come to life, as you become acquainted with the grounds and buildings. Imagine what it felt like to awaken to the signals of rough seas and a ship in distress. Learn what a bit of day-to-day life was like for these valiant men.

By 1901, there were about sixty lifesaving stations along the Great Lakes. The need was great for the station at Sleeping Bear Point, because of the Manitou passage, the channel between the Manitou islands and the mainland. By the turn of the century, the passage became a heavily traveled shipping lane for ships sailing between Chicago and the Straits of Mackinaw. Seamen preferred this channel rather than the open waters of Lake Michigan for several reasons. First, the distance was shorter. Also, there was a harbor of refuge on South Manitou Island, which provided an important natural harbor between Chicago and the Manitou passage, a distance of 220 miles. This was and still can be a very dangerous passage. The currents are coming from all different directions, which creates turbulence, and there are many rocky places. Many shipwrecks occurred. However, since November of 1960, when the *Francisco Morazan* shipwrecked, none have occurred.

The Sleeping Bear Point station was typical of the many lifesaving stations both along the Great Lakes and the Atlantic coast. Each day of the week had a certain activity, such as boat practice, beach rescue drill, or "resuscitation of the apparently drowned." These men kept constant watch for ships in danger. On foggy days and at night the men walked beach patrol. Constant vigilance on their part prevented many accidents from occurring, and enabled prompt assistance when one did occur.

Over the years, as radio, radar, and helicopter technological development occurred, the need for lifesaving stations was reduced. The Sleeping Bear Point station was closed during World War II. In 1971,

South Manitou Island Light

it served briefly as a visitor center for the newly established Sleeping Bear Dunes National Lakeshore. In 1982 and 1983, the site underwent historic renovation. Today, the grounds and the buildings still resemble their 1931 appearance. The interior of the boat house and the crew's bedroom were restored to appear as they did in the early 1900s. Official dedication of the museum took place on Coast Guard Day, August 4, 1984.

GRAND TRAVERSE LIGHTHOUSE.

The Grand Traverse Lighthouse is at the tip of the peninsula, in Leelanau State Park between Lake Michigan and Grand Traverse Bay, nine miles north of Northport. On July 2, 1851, President Millard Fillmore authorized the building of this lighthouse, called Cathead Point. Vessels heading into the bay needed it to safely round the shoals at the tip of the peninsula. The boats heading down the lake to the straits needed it as a reference point.

Construction began in 1852 on a circular tower east of the existing structure. This tower had a brief life. According to some accounts, the wave action of Lake Michigan threatened the structure.

The present brick lighthouse was built in 1864. It is listed on the National Register of Historic Places. The foundation was built from bricks reclaimed from the first lighthouse. The light tower, a square structure 7½ feet on each side, extended from the gabled roof of the dwelling. The light and the keeper's residence were renovated in 1916, which gave the brick structure its present appearance.

Passing schooners and steamers were alerted to the rocky shore by the beacon's warning lights beaming across the waters of Lake Michigan. The elements threw a beam of light fifteen miles out. The lens was originally a fourth order Fresnel lens imported from France (first order Fresnel lens are the largest at twelve feet). United States lighthouses were outfitted with Fresnel lens starting in 1852. This type of lens was developed in 1822 by French physicist Augustin Jean Fresnel. It has many panels of polished glass surrounding a light source to refract the light and focus it out over the water. In the early days, the lens was lit by a kerosene lamp, but later was powered by electricity. The lens is on display in the museum.

In 1899, a brick building was erected to house the steam fog signal. It sounded its warning for many miles. A brick "oil house" was constructed. The equipment is gone but the buildings have survived the many changes of navigational history.

Since 1852, the light has been tended by a succession of fourteen keepers. For over a century, the keepers handled the lens with meticulous care.

The Coast Guard abandoned the lighthouse and built a steel skeleton in 1972 near the old buildings. Daytime navigation is now aided by red and white markers on this tower. There is also an automated foghorn eight miles offshore.

The United States government turned over thirty acres to the State of Michigan in 1932, for use as a state park. This helped protest the lighthouse from vandalism.

The lighthouse is lovingly cared for by the Grand Traverse Lighthouse Foundation established in 1986. A great catalyst to the foundation came in the person of Doug McCormick, who as a youngster cared for the light with his father between 1923 and 1938. He is proudly refurbishing the premises for others to come and enjoy. His great love and knowledge of the lighthouse and its rich maritime history is evident.

The museum presently charges no admission but donations are gladly accepted. There is a small but growing gift shop. The profits help preserve the Grand Traverse Lighthouse Foundation grounds and buildings.

SOUTH MANITOU ISLAND LIGHTHOUSE.

Completion of the Erie Canal in 1826 rapidly increased the development of commercial navigation on the Great Lakes. The lighthouse at South Manitou Island was needed to mark the entrance to the Manitou Passage, the most important route for vessels traveling the 300 mile length of Lake Michigan.

Nineteenth-century steamers consumed one to three hundred cords of wood on each of the thirty to thirty-five trips they made yearly through the Great Lakes. The wooding station and the natural harbor made this a welcome island. Here the light beckoned to the passing ships. A much needed light, indeed, in violent weather.

The first wooden lighthouse was built in 1840. In 1858, the U.S. Lighthouse Establishment recognized the need for greater safety. The wooden lighthouse was replaced by a two-story brick residence with a thirty-five-foot tower on top. The tower housed a fourth order Fresnel lens. A fog signal building was added and both structures still stand today.

Increased shipping traffic brought even more changes, and in 1871 a hundred-foot tower was built. A third order Fresnel lens was installed with a three-wick lamp that had a range of eighteen miles. A passageway was added connecting the tower to the keeper's dwelling. In 1875, the first steam fog signal on Lake Michigan was installed, replacing the fog bell. After the vigilance of seventeen keepers and thirty assistant keepers, the light was abandoned by the Coast Guard in 1958.

The lighthouse is widely acclaimed to be on of the most beautiful on all the Great Lakes. South Manitou Island is a part of the Sleeping Bear Dunes National Lakeshore. The island is maintained by the National Park Service and is open to the public.

NORTH MANITOU ISLAND LIGHTHOUSE.

A lighthouse existed on North Manitou Island from 1898 through 1935. Time and Lake Michigan's mighty waves have claimed most of it; there are a few crumbling remains.

SOUTH FOX ISLAND LIGHTHOUSE.

On probably one of the prettiest islands of the Great Lakes. South Fox Island lies about 16½ miles north-northwest of Cathead Point, making it the most isolated island in Lake Michigan. The island is Crescent shaped and has 11½ miles of shoreline and twenty-one hundred acres of nearly unspoiled wilderness. There is some evidence that both North and South Fox Islands were used by the French explorers in the early 1600s.

South Fox has no natural harbor. A ship could hide behind the island from approaching storms. A lighthouse was erected in 1867 on the southern tip of the island.

During the summer of 1991 Doug McCormick, now caretaker of

the Grand Traverse Lighthouse, filmed South Fox and her light. His father, James McCormick, was keeper there between 1916 and 1921. Mr. McCormick reflects that the once grand light is in "horrible condition, overgrown with trees, one even growing through the roof, vandalized, but still solid." Mr. McCormick fondly recollects his happy boyhood memories of life on South Fox Island.

Behind the lighthouse is a grave belonging to a Civil War vet. The grave simply says "Post 899." Beside it lies another grave marked for a dog named "Leader."

NORTH MANITOU SHOAL LIGHT.

Extending several miles between the islands and the Leelanau peninsula lie the North Manitou Shoals, a dangerous area ships needed to avoid. This "crib light" was constructed in 1935, making the South Manitou Light obsolete. National Lakeshore Ranger Bill Herd explains that crib is a slang term for this light, a permanently anchored structure that resembles a crib to sailors. Preceding this construction, the Lighthouse Establishment in 1907 recommended that the shoal off North Manitou Island's southern tip be marked by a lightship. Bill Herd continues to explain that a lightship is a boat that serves as a lighthouse. In 1910 Lightship No. 56 was transferred from White Shoals at the Straits of Mackinaw. Throughout the navigational history, from April to early December, the lightship along with the North Manitou Island Lighthouse, marked the shoal until 1927.

In 1927, Lightship No. 89 assumed the vigil and was eventually replaced by the permanent, radar-controlled steel-framed structure that still lights the way through this hazardous area.

The U.S. Coastguard maintains this fully automated light. It is known as "The Crib." The North Manitou Shoal Light was the last manned offshore light station on the Great Lakes. It became automated by the Coast Guard in 1980.

Seasons of the Maritime

BEACH-COMBING FOR SHIPWRECKS.

Many ships (no one knows the exact number) have been lost in the turbulent waters of the Manitou passage. The remains of at least eighty ships lie within the Manitou passage area according to a marker outside the Sleeping Bear Point Coast Guard Station Maritime Museum. Thought to be the first shipwreck in the area, though undocumented, is the *Free Trader*, in 1835. Later wrecks include the *Black Hawk,* also undocumented, which disappeared with all hands on deck in 1847; the *Westmoreland,* in 1854, with seven survivors and seventeen reported missing and an unconfirmed rumor of gold cargo aboard; the *Gilbert Mollison,* which foundered in Good Harbor Bay in 1873, all hands lost; and the *Francisco Morazan,* in 1960, all fourteen aboard saved. Today, divers explore these historic shipwreck sights in the Manitou Passage State Underwater Preserve. This preserve was established in 1988 to conserve the archeological and historic value of these shipwrecks.

It is not necessary to be a diver to explore these remains. The same natural forces of wind and waves that caused most of these wrecks can quickly uncover a sight buried in sand for over a hundred years. The sight may be visible for a few days or possibly, a few weeks. Beach-combing for shipwrecks is like a treasure hunt for history.

It's important to realize that shipwrecks are the sight of past tragedies. Be careful not to make them the sight of a current one. Use extreme caution, for wet timbers are slippery. Metal spikes and iron pins can cause serious injury. Even small waves have the power to push an unwary wader onto timbers and spikes. Take only pictures! Removing any of these shipwrecks is not only a violation of federal law but also deprives other visitors of the opportunity to enjoy these treasured sights.

Much of the wood you will find along the beach is from land structures, such as docks, break walls, steps, and boat houses. Land structures have straight edges and square corners. There usually are no straight lines or square corners on a ship. A ship's timbers are curved and have strong metal fasteners every few inches. Timbers of white oak are black when wet, and white when dry. Metal fasteners, such as spikes, rods, pegs, and bolts, are sometimes found. Hardware occasionally washes ashore too, such as iron rings, chain, cleats, and hawser pipes.

What part of a ship is it? Finding the pieces to a shipwreck is much like a puzzle. To determine what part you have found, you need to have some idea how wooden ships were built. The upper part of the vessel cabins and deck were lightly constructed of pine and nails and were easily destroyed by Lake Michigan. The strong timbered hull usually broke apart between the bottom and the sides at the turn of the bilge or about waterline. The bottom of the hull had extra large timbers running perpendicular to the ribs. These are the keel (outside) and keelson (inside). The sides had planking on the ribs. The planking usually decreases in thickness as it goes up. The sides may have wood or metal knees or braces to support the deck beams.

Methods of building wooden ships changed little when shipwrecks were occurring along the Manitou passage. Thus, it is very difficult to date a shipwreck from just the part discovered along the beach. However, there are several rules of thumb. The early ships had wooden pegs as well as iron pins. Later ships used more iron bracing than the earlier ones. Bolts and nuts found on a piece usually indicate a later ship. The wooden boats that were wrecked along the Lakeshore were constructed between 1829 and 1898.

Whether you can narrow a find to a few possible shipwrecks is only a small part of the enjoyment of beach-combing. Enjoy your find, take pictures, and carefully explore. Study the construction method. Make a drawing. Also, please let the park visitor center, in Empire know of your find.

You may view the shipwreck *Francisco Morazan*, still above water on the south side of South Manitou Island. She ran aground on November 29, 1960.

Recommended reading to find out more about the wrecks include George Weeks's *Sleeping Bear: Yesterday and Today* and Steve Harold's *Shipwrecks of the Sleeping Bear.*

Seasons of the Maritime

PIRACY.

Pirates on the Great Lakes? There are various stories. Early piracy was blamed on the Strang group, Mormons who lived on Beaver Island. However, piracy could also be attributed to the residents on the mainland. John Norton Rohr, in *Some Other Day* by the Empire Heritage Group, recalls piracy in the Empire area. His grandparents came to Empire in 1857. Apparently, the pirates had control in the area of their farm, and his grandparents were afraid to speak against them.

A man named Perry had his own set-up. He would head north on the dune, get halfway up, and set a brightly lit lantern just past dusk. This drew the boats off their course. After a boat wrecked on shore, Perry would loot it of all its valuables and stash them in the cellar for the black market.

NORTHWEST MICHIGAN MARITIME MUSEUM. Presently under proposal in new headquarters in Empire is the Northwest Michigan Maritime Museum. The museum focuses on 282 miles of the Bottomlands preserve. Plans are underway to renovate a 1910 livery building to house the museum. The museum was formerly in Frankfort.

MANITOU PASSAGE STATE UNDERWATER PRESERVE (see chapter 11).

There is so much more to discover about the seasons of the maritime. It's the intent of this chapter to whet your appetite to come to the Leelanau and discover more of her rich maritime heritage in a land closely linked to the Great Lakes, both in seasons past and those to come.

9

The Sleeping Bear Dunes National Shoreline

Sleeping Bear, where is she now?
Can one make out her shaggy brow?
Or how long do legends live?
Do they have a time limit to give?

    On the northwestern shore of Michigan's Lower Peninsula lies the Sleeping Bear Dunes National Lakeshore, one of the most breathtakingly beautiful areas in the world. In 1970, Congress designated seventy-two thousand acres for the Sleeping Bear Dunes National Lakeshore.
    The region is hilly, fringed with massive coastal sand dunes and crystal-clear azure blue lakes. The landscape is diverse. The rugged bluffs are as high as 460 feet above Lake Michigan's pounding surf, paralleled with quiet birch-lined streams and dense beech-maple forests. Several miles offshore lie the North and South Manitou islands, tranquil and secluded, with a rich legacy to behold.

The National Lakeshore

In each of the seasons, the Sleeping Bear National Lakeshore has much to offer: from the first wildflowers in spring, peeping out from under wet, fallen leaves; to the heat of summer, when the beautiful, clear waters offer comfort and relief; to fall with its majestic dance of color; and then winter, with its quiet beauty and deep snows to enjoy.

The sunsets over Sleeping Bear country are magnificent in all seasons. Many traditionally come to the beach for this wonderful gift of nature; afterward, they light a private camp fire and enjoy the night air while listening to the gently lapping waves.

Chippewa Indian Legend of the Sleeping Bear told and retold for many years is the legend of Sleeping Bear. Long ago in the land that today is Wisconsin, a mother bear and her two cubs were driven into Lake Michigan by a raging forest fire. They swam and swam, but the cubs tired, and lagged farther and farther behind. Mother bear finally reached the opposite shore and climbed to the top of a bluff to watch and wait for her offspring. The cubs had drowned. Today Sleeping Bear, a solitary dune in the lakeshore, marks the legendary spot where the mother bear still waits. Her hapless cubs are the two Manitou islands. Besides the legend, for thousands of visitors each year, the Sleeping Bear Dunes offer a wealth of opportunity to enjoy the outdoors. Many come to climb or to savor sweeping views of land and water from the roadway. Others come to hike the trails where they find a great variety of plants, birds, and other wildlife. Beach-combing is an easy activity while visiting here. In winter, there is so much for the cross-country skier to traverse: Deep in the woods, meadows are covered with freshly fallen snow; along bluffs there are breathtaking views over Lake Michigan and the other inland lakes.

The recreational activities of the Sleeping Bear Dunes National Lakeshore are many. About one and a half million people visit the park each year. To become acquainted with these activities, please see chapter 11.

HISTORY COMES TO LIFE

The history of the Sleeping Bear Dunes is an exciting avenue to discover. Evidence exists that the area was inhabited by prehistoric people over three thousand years ago. More recently, the Ottawa and Chippewa, tribes of the western Great Lakes Indians, migrated seasonally here. Their familiarity with the area gave rise to the legends that enrich the mystique and aura of Sleeping Bear history. The first Europeans to penetrate this wilderness were the French in the early 1600s. By the late 1600s, "l'ours qui dort" (the Sleeping Bear) was a well-known landmark to the French. Many assume that all of Sleeping Bear Point is the legendary "mother bear," but she is only the dark and shaggy mound on the south part of the point. This mound was very visible from offshore to approaching boats and looks like the shape of a shaggy bear. Because of time changing the geography of the area, this mound is less pronounced than in times past, perhaps starting the new legend, "Has the mother bear moved?" The French pioneered the fur-trading era, which continued into the nineteenth century and involved the French, English, and native Americans.

As the American frontier was expanding in the early 1800s, commercial shipping on the Great Lakes played a major role. Lake Michigan became a major trade route (see chapter 11). The Manitou passage proved to be an important shipping lane.

Biologic Diversity

Biologic diversity is critical in the health of the park. More important is how it reflects on a larger scale the earth, for all life is inextricably linked to all other life. The increase in population and subsequent development has reached a point where humans are displacing other species at a much higher rate than at any other time in the earth's history. As stability is lost, we lose the ability to survive environmental changes. The government tries to protect this natural variety by preserving large parts of land and striving to keep the air and water free of toxins. While at the park, you can help by refraining from disturbing native plants and animals. Take home pictures, memories, and any litter. This is precious land so please obey park rules and help preserve the beauty found here.

Habitats in the National Lakeshore

The habitats in the lakeshore are of four types: the dunes, meadows, forests, and wetlands. The terrain provides the setting for over seven hundred plant species.

Sand Dunes

The sand dunes are the product of a long and complex geologic and botanical history. The dunes were deemed so valuable that Congress set them aside as part of the National Park System. Thus, the area could be preserved and maintained for the enjoyment of people today and of generations to come. Visitors are encouraged to visit the dunes, but gently. If the only impact we leave behind is footprints in the sand, the next strong breeze will erase them and leave the dunes ready for others to enjoy.

A sand dune is a wind-deposited pile of sand composed of mineral and rock grains. For a sand dune to develop, there must be an abundant supply of sand, wind of sufficient strength, and a place for the sand to be deposited. Dunes are often associated with deserts, where lack of plant cover exposes the sand to wind. Here in the humid, temperate climate of Michigan, conditions in these coastal areas likewise favor the dunes. Glacial deposits provided the abundant sand, Lake Michigan the open expanse where prevailing winds pick up speed, and the leeward land mass provides a place where the sand can be deposited.

Dunes can be classified into four categories: beach dunes, perched dunes, falling dunes, and "de-perched" dunes, based on their location and mode of origin.

Active dunes gradually advance over the years. In time, trees and telephone poles become buried in drifting sand. A common question is, How fast are the dunes moving? The rate of movement varies from one place to another and one year to the next. At the Dune Climb the average rate of advance has been about four feet per year over the past few years. Although the movement of sand produces impressive changes, ultimately that movement may be limited by several factors, one being the stabilization of the dune by plant cover.

Beach grass, sand cherry, and cottonwood are among the first plants to appear. As the ensuing plant decay enriches the soil, conditions become favorable for other plants and eventually a forest may develop. This is known as plant succession.

Meadows

Open fields and meadows, with their array of grasses, herbs, and shrubs, are interspersed throughout the park. Most are the product of the past farming era. Some of the most visible species of plants are spotted knapweed, orange hawkweed, milkweed, common mullein, and black-eyed Susan. Over the years, brambles staghorn sumac, and other shrubby vegetation begin to move in as old orchards, pastures, and abandoned farm fields start their succession to a beech-maple climax forest.

The National Lakeshore

Forests

Inland from the beach and shrub zones, forests appear. Red and white pines and red oaks dominate this zone. There may be a combination of quaking and large-toothed aspens depending on soil conditions. Covering the forest floor are bracken fern, smooth aster, wintergreen, bunchberry (dwarf dogwood), blueberry, wild sarsaparilla, coreopsis, and an array of other colorful wildflowers. Most popular are the spring wildflowers found here. These include trillium, jack-in-the-pulpit, bloodroot, spring beauty, and hepatica. An excellent guide to identify these is *Michigan Wildflowers* in Color by Harry C. Lund.

The last stage in the succession process in the northeastern United States is the American beech and sugar maple climax forest. Climax vegetation is the vegetation cover that an area will maintain over time—if the area suffers no environmental impact, such as logging or forest fires. Other tree species found in the beech-maple forest association include basswood, ironwood, black cherry, white ash, and, in moister areas, yellow birch and hemlock.

Wetlands

Other plant communities exist in ponds, lakes, streams, bogs, swamps, and marshes. Wetlands are crucial in the maintenance and health of water resources and produce more wildlife and plants than any other Michigan habitat type. Of the twenty-three hundred native plants found in Michigan, half are wetland species. More than 25 percent of these are threatened or endangered. Wetland species account for much of our diversity, but many plants are disappearing from these areas. Over 75 percent of the original wetland area in Michigan has been filled, developed, or altered in some way. Species found in shallow water include arrowgrass, arrowhead, water smartweed, and bulrush. Near the water's edge one can find spearmint, marsh pea, sedges, and bugleweed, among others. Tree species found in or near the wetlands include white cedar, yellow birch, balsam fir, tamarack, American elm, and green ash.

Wildlife

Presently, the dunes are home to about forty-nine species of mammals; other species have been eradicated, largely because of human encroachment. Among these lost mammals are the marten, wolverine, timber wolf, cougar, lynx, elk, moose, and caribou. Some of the animals that still inhabit the park, such as the bobcat and black bear, are rare and seldom seen.

In the dunes, even a short walk will reveal signs of animals. Mice, deer, raccoons, and fox leave their tracks on the dunes. Sand cherry pits are an important food for the mice. They open the pits with their teeth and extract the kernel inside.

Old farm fields play host to woodchucks, foxes, and ground squirrels, who make their burrows in the soft earth. Moles leave evidence of their presence with ridges of raised earth as they dig their tunnels. Deer are plentiful and often seen feeding in open fields about dusk.

In the woods, old hollow trees are home for raccoons, opossum, and porcupines. Gray squirrels, seen in their black phase in the park, feed on the nuts of beech trees and oaks. Red squirrels favor the seeds of pine.

In the lakes, streams, and ponds, one can find beaver, muskrats, and mink. The presence of beaver can be seen by the cut trees near the water, as well as the lodges, dams, and canals. Muskrats make houses using cattails and other wetland vegetation. On rare occasions, river otter are seen in the park.

Native birds that reside in all four seasons include the ruffled grouse, the herring and the ringbilled gull, the hairy and downy woodpeckers, the blue jay, the black-capped chickadee, white-breasted nuthatch, cedar waxwing, and the house sparrow.

Occasionally you may spot a common loon, great blue heron, whistling swan, Canada goose, the wood duck, the common golden-eyed duck, red-tailed hawk, the kestrel, the American coot, the killdeer, common flicker, yellow-bellied sapsucker, great crested flycatcher, alder flycatcher, brown thrasher, black and white warbler, chestnut-sided warbler, brown-headed cowbird, evening grosbeak, American goldfinch, tree sparrow, and the swamp sparrow.

Guidelines on Wildlife

Do not feed or interact with wildlife in any way. Wild creatures should be allowed to live undisturbed. Be careful when driving, especially at night. Many animals are nocturnal and are difficult to see along the roadsides. Deer-auto accidents are frequent in this area.

Wild animals may carry diseases harmful to humans. For example, raccoons harbor a roundworm that is hazardous, especially to children. Stay away from animals and their scats, for your own safety. Pamphlets on the biology and checklists for spotting wildlife are available at park headquarters.

HISTORIC GLEN HAVEN

(This sketch of historic Glen Haven is adapted from information in *Sleeping Bear: Yesterday and Today,* by George Weeks.)

Glen Haven is perhaps the best preserved example of a frontier wooding station and steamboat stopover on the Great Lakes. It is listed on the National Register of Historic Places as a turn-of-the-century lumbering town. C. C. McCarty was the first man to capitalize on the area's bounty by building a sawmill and inn in 1857. This inn existed for 115 years, closing in 1972. He called this new settlement Sleeping Bearville. Later it was changed to its present name. Glen Haven provided the most sheltered spot in the area, offering a deep-water approach when adequate harbors were nearly nonexistent.

Instrumental to Glen Haven's significance was David Henry Day. He was coined "King David of the north"; though no king, he was certainly highly esteemed among the pioneers, before his death in 1928. He was the first chairman of the State Park Commission. The Traverse City Record-Eagle stated: "D. H. Day did more than any other man to make Leelanau County the producer it is today."

In 1881, Day bought the village of Glen Haven. At this time, according to an 1881 plat map, Glen Haven had eleven buildings, including an inn, school, wagon shop, and a store. There was a granary and root cellar to the east. To the north stood an icehouse, a necessary building because the cutting of ice on Glen Lake was a major activity in the winter. The inn, known as The Sleeping Bear Inn, is on the National Register of Historic Places.

D. H. Day had far more grandiose dreams for Glen Haven. According to National Park Service Historian Cockrell, he wanted to transform Glen Haven "into the most elaborate and exclusive resort in the United States."

During the mid-twentieth century, the Sleeping Bear Dunesmobile Rides out of Glen Haven introduced thousands to the dunes. These rides were ended in 1978.

Day's dream for a resort was never realized. The National Park Service bought all of the village by the mid-1970s. Besides being one of the best preserved cordwood stations in the Great Lakes, Glen Haven has the distinction of being on Michigan's shortest state highway, quarter-mile-long M-209.

MANITOU ISLANDS

These two beautiful islands rise like jewels out of majestic Lake Michigan. Just as in seasons past, the Manitou islands are a great attraction for summer visitors. In fall, North Manitou Island is full of deer hunters. But beware! Lake Michigan, at times so passive, can reap a torrential display with waves to ten feet, keeping one stranded on the Manitous for an extra day or two, or even longer. You can rely on the Manitou Transit to supply completely safe passage, and when necessary, a delayed cruise. Come prepared for that possibility. For cruise information see chapter 10.

The Manitou islands were named by the native American Indian. The term "manitou" to the Ottawa stood for the unseen power, or spirit, that every being in their world was said to possess. Some accounts have stated that the islands were not visited by the Indians for fear of "evil spirits." However, evidence indicates that they used these islands seasonally. The Indian legend of the Sleeping Bear explains that these two islands were formed from the two cubs swimming after the mother bear and mark the spot where they drowned. The Great Spirit Manitou created these islands.

Today, when one visits these islands, one catches glimpses of another era. Some of the old farms still are standing and the cemeteries also give evidence of their past. It is thought that somewhere in the mid-1800s the islands' first residents began to settle there.

SOUTH MANITOU ISLAND

South Manitou Island is composed of 5,260 acres, and is eight miles square. It is sixteen miles west of Leland and seven and a half miles north of Sleeping Bear Point. According to South Manitou Island historian Myron H. Vent, because of the island's strategic location, it became the first place of settlement and commerce in the region. The island's natural resources have been used by various interests, including the lumbermen, farmers, shipping, the Life-Saving and Lighthouse services, and Coast Guard in seasons past. Today, it attracts campers and general day visitors.

The first settlers of South Manitou served the early steamers. They operated a wooding station and built a lighthouse, which was greatly needed. The earliest settlers recorded on the island were William N. Burton and his family, about 1835. He became the first lighthouse keeper in 1840. Its last year-round residents were Ed and Esther Riker in 1974 after the National Park Service bought the farm where they lived and worked. Of the two islands, South Manitou, being less primitive, receives the most visitors. First stop at the island is at the Visitors Center, in the old Island Post Office in the center of the village. It houses interesting exhibits that portray the human and natural history of the island.

Next on the agenda, an island tour, offered by the crew that brought you over. They are specially trained to interpret the island's natural and cultural history. South Manitou's personality will unfold with tales of human history. Some tours focus on natural history as you hike through lush undercover, which contains hundreds of wildflowers to add to the enchantment. Others are to the top of the perched dunes for a different aspect of the island's topography.

South Manitou Island has only ten species of mammals, compared with about forty species on the mainland. These include chipmunk, shrew, fox squirrel, snowshoe hare, deer mouse, fox, and four species of bat. The small size of the island and its isolation prohibit a diverse mammal population. There are four open-air vehicles available for the tour, so customized tours can be arranged for those with special interests and abilities. Tours are set up on board during the cruise over. Each tour takes about an hour and a half.

Experience a visit to the Valley of the Giants, in the southwest corner of the island. It is a grove of virgin white cedar trees, including the world's record white cedar measuring 17.

6 feet in circumference and over 90 feet tall. Some trees are more than five hundred years old. They escaped the lumberjack's ax, probably because of their location.

A special sight at the island is the wreck of the *Francisco Morazan*. This was a Liberian freighter, which ran aground in a snowstorm in November 1960. It is not advisable for persons to explore the deck of this wreck. It has proven to be extremely dangerous. Fires set by vandals have made the wood very deceiving, for what looks like a solid surface could very well not be. It is a nesting area for gulls and cormorants, making it a most scenic site.

Mention must be made of beautiful Florence Lake at the southern end of the island, described as a "sparkling jewel, cuddled in the bosom of her Mother Isle." Florence Lake was always "alive and dancing when caressed by summer breezes that send countless wavelets shoreward, to lap softly on her sandy shore. . . . Dear to my memory are her countless moods, ever changing with the passing seasons." These words were first written in The *South Manitou Story* by

Gerald E. Crowner, a surf man at the South Manitou Station between 1926 and 1928. Fitting words indeed.

A ranger station is on the island. It is housed in the former Coast Guard Station in the village. The rangers are there to help you enjoy your visit and protect the island resources. All emergencies and requests for assistance are to be reported to the rangers. In an emergency the Ranger Station can be reached from the mainland at (616) 334-3976. There are picnic tables here, but you may enjoy your picnic lunch anywhere on the island. You must bring your own lunch. No food is available for purchase on the island.

Camping is available at three locations: the Bay, the Weather Station, and the Popple campgrounds. Outhouses, fire pits, and water are available. National Park regulations state low impact camping only! Park Ranger Bill Herd says low impact camping means "you leave no trace that you've been there." This is to minimize the human impact on this beautiful island's fragile resources. No transportation is available to you campers so pack it in and travel light! Food gear should be stored in hard containers or hung from a line to discourage the chipmunks and raccoons. Be sure to come prepared to stay and extra day or more in case lake conditions prevent safe travel back to the mainland. Campers must register on a free back country permit, available from the park rangers. Because back country camping is an individual experience, most sites are designed to hold a maximum of four campers. There are several larger group campsites available, each designed to hold twenty-five campers. Please call park headquarters in Empire for reservations. The telephone number is (616) 326-5134.

NORTH MANITOU ISLAND

North Manitou Island was acquired by the National Park Service in 1984. Before that, it was in the hands of private ownership, with no history of public use. Travel on the island is by foot only.

North Manitou Island comprises fifteen thousand acres, with twenty miles of shoreline. It is just over seven miles long and four miles wide. From Leland it is a twelve-mile boat ride. Rugged and remote, the island contains a wide array of topography, including wooded bluffs and sandy dunes. Lake Manitou is in the northern midsection of the island.

To the west of Lake Manitou, the topography becomes rugged as you approach the west and the northwest bluffs. The bluffs become incised and steep between Swenson's and the Pot Holes. Its three hundred-foot-high face is deeply gullied by erosion.

The island has seen the heyday of the lumbering era, has known farming, has watched a lighthouse and the U.S. Life-Saving Service come and go, and has been a true escape for summer residents seeking solitude. Today, little remains of seasons past. The lighthouse, at the south end of the island, is a pile of bricks and a small shack that once was the keeper's home. A few buildings are scattered throughout the island. Some are in obvious decay, others appear usable. Many of these buildings are decrepit and are dangerous to enter. Small cemeteries are another sign that people once lived here. The village area is composed of many houses once used as summer homes or hunting lodges. The old Coast Guard Station is in fairly good condition. An old sawmill and a cherry barn mark past activities. An abandoned airstrip gives evidence of more modern human attempts.

On the west end of the island, all that remains of the once-booming town of Crescent is an open field and an old barn; Crescent is now a ghost town.

In 1927, five male and two female deer were introduced to the island with the hope that they would multiply. As usual, when man tries to rearrange nature, things go awry. By 1981, two thousand animals were counted during the fall and winter. This extremely large deer population-density caused overbrowsing, which gave the island's woods a parklike appearance. The lack of small herbs and young seedlings poses a great threat to the composition of the island. As old trees die no new ones take their place. Thus, an unusually high deer population will totally change the island's vegetation in the next thirty to forty years. Through careful management of the herd by hunting and other measures, it is hoped that the vegetation will regenerate and restore the natural balance of the plant community on North Manitou. Hunts have been held annually since 1985, reducing the deer population to about four hundred animals.

The piping plover nests on the secluded beaches of this island. This small pale bird has one black neck band and a soft, two-note call that is organlike. This is an endangered species. North Manitou Island has one of the few nesting areas in the Great Lakes region. The Dimmicks Point area is closed to hikers May 1 through August 15, so as not to disturb their nesting.

North Manitou Island is a designated wilderness. Camping is allowed both at the designated village site, and throughout the island. Camping is a privilege here; please follow the set guidelines. Do not camp within sight of a trail, nor within three hundred feet of any water, including Lake Michigan, or other lakes, ponds, or streams. Pitch more than two tents per site, and with no more than four unrelated persons. Be prepared, if camping at the village, for a four- to five-mile hike to the site. Presently, the ferry is docking at the south side of the island. Plans for a new dock, scheduled to be opened in 1993, will greatly shorten the hike.

PIERCE STOCKING SCENIC DRIVE

Pierce Stocking Scenic Drive lies between Lake Michigan and Glen Lake. This scenic seven-and-a-half-mile road provides visitors the experience of area beauty, without leaving the car. The views to discover on this drive are panoramic. Memories of this area will stay with you.

The drive was named after a lumberman who developed it from 1967 until his death in 1976. Pierce Stocking spent his youth working as a lumberman in Michigan's great forests. He developed a self-taught knowledge of nature by spending much time in the woods he loved so much. He was awed by the views of the lakes and dunes and islands, and wanted to share this beauty with others. Thus was conceived the idea of a road to the top of the dunes. In 1977, the road became part of the Sleeping Bear Dunes National Lakeshore. A major road renovation took place in 1986. At the beginning of the drive, pamphlets are available to guide one through the drive. Twelve numbered points of interest are covered in the pamphlet.

Bicycling is permitted along the entire length of the drive. It is a challenging bike tour; be sure of your ability before starting. There are several steep uphill and downhill grades.

CAMPING, CROSS-COUNTRY SKIING, AND HIKING

Camping on the mainland and the many trails used for hiking and cross-country skiing are covered in chapter 11.

The National Lakeshore

10

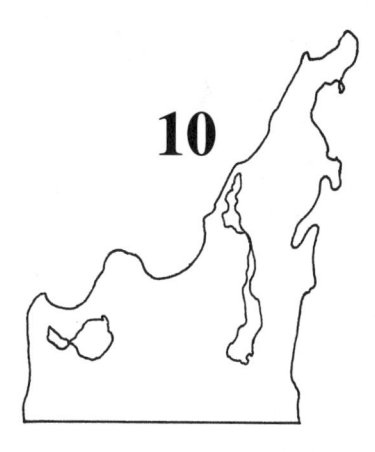

Fishing and Boating

Skim mirrored glass.
Pounce through mighty surf.
Fish her waters.
Walk sandy earth.

Seasonal changes of northern Michigan create a variety of fishing adventures for the beginning as well as experienced angler. There are ninety-eight miles of Great Lakes shoreline, forty-three inland lakes, and fifty-eight miles of streams in the Leelanau. The largest inland lake is South Lake Leelanau, 5,370 acres, followed by Big Glen, 4,865 acres, North Lake Leelanau, 2,950 acres, and Little Glen, 1,400 acres. Smaller lakes include Little Traverse Lake, Lime Lake, School Lake, and Bass Lake, among others.

Fish the waters of Lake Michigan and on West Grand Traverse Bay with your choice of many experienced charter captains or on your own. The cold, deep water is ideal for several delicious species of game fish, such as perch, brown trout, lake trout, steelhead, chinook, and coho salmon.

Traverse Bay hosts one of the state's best fisheries for

whitefish, an excellent eating fish that commonly weighs five pounds and better, and puts up a memorable battle! For a bigger fight, there's chinook salmon for deep-water trolling. The lake trout lurk deeply in these waters. It may appear that their numbers are reduced due to treaty-guaranteed Indian commercial fishing, but there's still lots of good fishing for them.

SPRING

In the spring the fish activity increases as the warming temperatures begin to occur. This brings in Lake Michigan steelhead trout (rainbow trout) upriver on their annual spawning run. On your own try the shallow rock-strewn points around the bay, which hold trophy-size smallmouth bass, described often as the best fighter that swims "inch for inch and pound for pound." There is also plenty of action with perch. In spring, try anchoring along the drop-offs, near shore. The use of two- to three-inch live minnows is a good tactic.

Game fish are seeking warmer waters now, and are found in the shallows and at the outlets of rivers and creeks. During this time drifting spawn-bag baits, or the casting of heavy spoons along the bottom, can pay off with chinook salmon. They are now beginning their summer-long body-building program before the fall spawning carries them inshore again to run upstream.

Panfish, such as bluegills, perch, and sunfish, can be caught on smaller lakes, for these fish feed heavily before spawning in early summer. Earthworms are usually used to catch bluegills and sunfish; live minnows can be used for perch.

SUMMER

Though trout fishing is possible in lesser streams, salmon fishing is rarely done is shallow waters after spring. Trolling with down riggers in deeper waters is more effective. Spoons fished deep by means of down riggers take plenty of lakers. Lake trout can be located by a search for cold waters (forty-eight to fifty-two degrees), which they prefer.

Use the same rule of thumb for fishing chinook salmon in summer. They are most active in about fifty-four-degree water. For a handsome payoff, keep your lures where the warm water breaks off abruptly to cooler temperatures. Many types of lures have been developed to catch Great Lakes salmon. However, long, light spoons or wobbling cut plugs seem to be the two favorites for trolling.

The summer heat brings bass and pike fishing on many inland lakes. Artificial bait—spoons and plugs—provides most of the action. Bass-fishing season opens on the Saturday of Memorial Day weekend. Don't overlook smallmouth bass fishing. Some of the most popular baits are minnow-imitating plugs, live minnows, and small crank-baits. Try fishing in depths of ten to twenty feet along the shoreline.

Whitefish generally are harder to find than catch in summer. The presence of other anchored boats is a good indication that they are hitting. You'll be more successful with heavy jigging spoons bounced near the bottom at depths up to 150 feet. Midwinter, use the same tactic when ice covers West Grand Traverse Bay.

AUTUMN

In the fall, repeat spring patterns, *releasing* lake trout unharmed if you catch them. The cooling temperatures and beautiful fall colors make it a pleasant time to fish. This is the time of the year when coho and chinook salmon make their spawning runs up tributary streams from Lake Michigan. If you are not an angler but still would like to see salmon as they run, come sight see at the river in historic Fishtown.

WINTER

Winter fishing is popular on Grand Traverse Bay and the inland lakes. If ice is to be formed on the bay, it should be formed by mid-February. Only twice in recent memory has Lake Michigan been frozen all the way across: the winters of 1936 and 1972. Ice or no ice, in a boat or a shanty, anglers will be found fishing for panfish, smelt, lake trout, whitefish, and pike. Stouthearted fishermen will be going after perch in thirty-foot depths. Favorite baits include grubs and minnows. Jig for whitefish in 30- to 150-foot depths using various spoons. Chum the hole with corn or salmon eggs for a better payoff. Jig the lures, varying the cadence until you find a pattern that works. No matter what the season fish are waiting in the waters of Leelanau for many hours of happy angling.

SPECIAL REGULATIONS AND WARNING

No special exceptions to statewide fishing rules apply to fishing in Grand Traverse Bay. Lake trout may be kept only between May 1 and August 15.

INDIAN FISHERY

It is important for boaters in Michigan waters to understand the rights of treaty fishing. This is essential if state and tribal fishers are to successfully and peaceably pursue their lawful rights to fish in these waters. Ottawa and Chippewa bands have depended on fishing the Great Lakes for food and income since long before the Europeans came. Their fishing rights were retained in treaties of 1820, 1836, and 1855. In 1985, after several years of discussion and litigation, tribes and state and federal governments successfully negotiated a settlement. This agreement defines exclusive fishing zones for state and tribal fishers, which are jointly managed by the tribes and state. Judge Fox reminds us, "The mere passage of time has not eroded and cannot erode the rights guaranteed by solemn treaties that both sides pledge on their honor to uphold." Warning: The Michigan Department of Natural Resources has issued a public health advisory, included in the fishing regulations, warning about eating certain amounts and kinds of fish from Lake Michigan and its tributaries, as well as inland lakes, because of contaminants, such as PCBs, mercury, and dioxin. Check the regulations for details.

EMERGENCY SERVICES

On-water emergencies in Grand Traverse Bay are handled by the United States Coast Guard's Charlevoix Station (616) 547-2541 or

Fishing and Boating

2565.

Hospital services are in Traverse City. Call the Michigan State Police post in Traverse City at (616) 946-4646, or Leelanau County Sheriff at (616) 941-4411.

BOATING AND SAILING

The Leelanau peninsula is just that: a body of land surrounded on three sides by Lake Michigan and Grand Traverse Bay's beautiful waters. The opportunities for boaters are limited only by the time you have to spend. Many experienced sailors say that these waters provide some of the finest sailing in the world. Whether you own a boat or not, sailing is possible for all who wish to experience the lakes. From slips available for a few hours to a marina condo to buy, from renting a jet-ski or canoe to going out for a two-week sail on one of the tall ships—whatever your "water pleasure," you can find it here!

ELMWOOD TOWNSHIP MARINA (616) 946-5464. Transient moorings, seasonal slips, gasoline, telephone pay station, water, electricity, rest rooms, harbormaster, haul-out facilities, and holding tank pump-out. Near Traverse City on West Grand Traverse Bay.

LELAND TOWNSHIP HARBOR (616) 256-9132. Transient slips, gasoline and diesel fuel, water, electricity, rest rooms, shower facilities, harbor master (6:30 a.m.-10:00 p.m.), holding tank pump-out, and VHF-FM monitor channels 16 and 19. On Lake Michigan in Leland.

SUTTONS BAY MARINA (616) 271-6703. Transient slips, gasoline, water, electricity, rest rooms, shower facilities, harbormaster (7:00 a.m.-9:00 p.m.), swimming beach, holding tank pump-out, launch facilities, and VHF-FM monitor channel 16. Thirteen miles north of Traverse City on Suttons Bay.

NORTHPORT-DAME MARINA (616) 386-5182. Transient slips, gasoline and diesel fuel, water, electricity, rest rooms, shower facilities, harbormaster, holding tank pump-out, launch ramp, and VHF-

FM monitor channel 16. Thirty miles north of Traverse City on Northport Bay.

LELAND TOWNSHIP HARBOR (616) 386-5182. Transient slips, gasoline, water, electricity, rest rooms, shower facilities, harbormaster (7:00 a.m. -9:00 p.m.), holding tank pumpout, and VHF-FM monitor channels 16 and 19. On Lake Michigan in Leland.

CHARTERS

Leland has been a commercial fishing port since before the turn of the century, according to Capt. Bill Carlson, whose family has been in the business since the early 1880s. For sportfishing, the area has been a major fishing port since the 1960s. At that time lake trout were reintroduced and salmon introduced to Lake Michigan. Charters provide a means for the sportfishermen and others to enjoy the waters. Many captains offer cruises to explore the islands, sunset cruises, bed-and-breakfast cruises, dinner cruises, and ten-day trips.

One of the largest fish ever caught in the area was caught in 1989 by Captain Carlson during "The Real Peoples Derby," a statewide fishing tournament. His catch was a king salmon that weighed 34 lb., 12 oz. His prize? Fourteen thousand dollars! In 1991, he was successful at reeling in a 32-lb. king salmon.

The charter season generally lasts between May and September. Besides king salmon you can go after steelhead, lake trout, and perch. Charter captains are booked by the half day and full day; the full day is recommended because once you're out there experiencing the excitement you'll want to stay out there! Most charter boats can accommodate up to six passengers and most supply all gear needed (you are responsible for your food and beverages). It is an appreciated courtesy to bring food and beverages for the captain and crew, generally speaking. As for weather changes, keep in touch with your captain if any lake warnings are in effect. Make your reservations early; these guys are busy!The following charters are docked at the

Fishing and Boating

Leland Harbor, in Fishtown.

CARLSON FISHERIES (616) 256-9801. Box 406, Leland, MI 49654. Capt. Bill Carlson runs the 28-ft. *Double Trouble.*

FISHTOWN CHARTER SERVICE (616) 256-9639. Box 133, Leland, MI 49654. Capts. James Munoz and Ed Peplinski run the 30-ft. *Carol Dee* and the 28-ft. *Sea Witch.* Their charter service is the oldest sportfishing charter out of Leland.

INFINITY CHARTERS (616) 256-9159; dock (616) 256-7625. 4501 Lakeview, Interlochen, MI 49643. Capt. John Lindenau runs the 29-ft. *Infinity.*

NORTHWEST CHARTERS (616) 946-2204; boat (616) 256-7750. 10013 S. Lakeview Road, Traverse City, MI 49684. Capt. Scott Anderson on board with his 28-ft. *Far Fetched.*

SEA DOG CHARTERS (616) 946-2204; dock (616) 256-9681. 7427 Pinewood Court, Traverse City, MI 49684. Capt. Steve Otterbein runs the *Sea Dog.* He has added perch fishing (spring and fall only) to his charters.

WHITECAP CHARTERS (616) 256-7457; dock (616) 256-7535. Box 109, Leland, MI 49654. Capt. Jack Duffy runs the 26-ft. *White Cap.* He has fished on the Great Lakes since 1966, and has been fully licensed as a charter captain annually since 1972.

There are many other charters available, on Lake Michigan and West Grand Traverse Bay. Inquire locally.

SAILING CHARTERS

A tall ship, as she graces the waters surrounding the Leelanau, is an admirable sight. Even more exciting is to experience sailing one firsthand! There are three tall ships most commonly glimpsed: the *Malabar,* the *Manitou,* and the *Madeline.* The first two take passengers on daily sails, windjammer trips, and are floating bed-and-breakfast places. The *Madeline* is a dockside museum giving tours from the Clinch Park Marina in Traverse City. The *Malabar* was included in a

Fishing and Boating

special National Geographic television program on the Great Lakes in 1990, entitled "Great Lakes, Fragile Seas." The *Malabar* and the *Manitou* host a variety of educational programs for the Inland Seas Education Association at different times during the season.

The tall ships and the brave men who sailed them literally shaped this region. They contributed a tremendous amount of the history and folklore to this entire maritime region during the mid-1800s. We can give much credit to the men and women who contribute so much of their time, effort, and knowledge to preserving this rich maritime history and making it available to those who desire to learn more about this heritage.

TALL SHIP MALABAR

The *Malabar* was originally launched in Bath, Maine, in 1975 as a traditional two-masted, gaff-rigged, topsail schooner. When she is not out on the waters sailing, you will find her majestically moored at the end of an eight hundred-foot private pier. Her size is impressive, for she is one of the largest traditional sailing vessels on the Great Lakes. Her length is 105 feet, her beam 22 feet. A displacement (weight) of over a hundred tons ensures a safe and relaxing sail. Afternoon and sunset sails are available. She is a floating bed-and-breakfast place offering overnight accommodations. Adventurous guests stay in eight staterooms, which reflect the atmosphere of a mid-1800s-style windjammer.

THE SCHOONER MANITOU

The tall ship *Manitou* is a traditional two-masted topsail schooner, 114 feet in length. Built in the same traditional sense of the *Malabar*, the *Manitou* is 114 feet in length and has over three thousand square feet of sail. Up to twenty-four passengers can be accommodated in twelve double cabins. Offering three- and six-day cruises the *Manitou* takes you to various islands and sleepy coastal villages. You'll stop at places on Lake Michigan and Lake Huron for hiking and exploring; some of these places are untouched by civilization. The food aboard is fantastic; local specialties are emphasized, all home cooked in the ship's galley.

TRAVERSE TALL SHIP COMPANY (616) 941-2000. 13390 S. West-Bayshore Drive, Traverse City, MI 49684. Responsible for reservations for the *Malabar* and the *Manitou.*

THE *CYGNET* (616) 271-6637. P.O. Box 186, Suttons Bay, MI 49682. Sailing expeditions run by Tom Kelly, who also heads up The School Ship Program with the Inland Seas Education Association. The *Cygnet* is a thirty-five-foot ketch offering seamanship and sailing instruction. Half- and full-day sails.

CRUISING TO THE MANITOUS

George Tracy Grosvenenor began an island transit service in 1918 with the *Lawrence,* which had been operated as an island ferry by John Paetchow. For much of the twentieth century, the Grosvenor family has provided this service to the islands, which is the only public link. The vessels used for the one-and-a-half-hour trips are the *Mishe Mokwa* and the *Manitou Isle.*

MANITOU ISLAND TRANSIT (616) 256-9061 or (616) 271-4217. P.O. Box 591, Leland, MI 49654. Ticket office in Fishtown at the Port Hole. There is a special "Cocktail Cruise" along the coast of the Leelanau and the Manitou passage. Special charter trips are also available for clubs and groups.

CHARTERED BOAT ACCESS TO THE MANITOUS (616) 326-5134. Licensed charter boat captains have access to the islands if they have a valid commercial use license from the park superintendent. A list of those operators available for hire can be obtained by calling the headquarters for the Sleeping Bear Dunes National Lakeshore at the above number.

BOATS, TACKLE SHOPS, BAIT, AND SUPPLIES

THE SPORTSMAN SHOP (616) 334-3872. M-22, Glen Arbor, MI 49636. A complete tackle shop, offering marine electronics, live bait, Alumacraft boats. Friendly and honest fishing information.

BAY WEST TACKLE (616) 946-5355. 12815 Cherry Bend Road, Traverse City, MI 49684. Specializes in fishing tackle and live bait, marine accessories and supplies. Repair. Open seven days year-round.

THE COMPASS SPORTS CENTRE (616) 386-5212. 119 Waukazoo, Northport, MI 49670. Fishing tackle and bait. Marine accessories and fishing licenses.

WOODY'S MARINE SUPPLIES (616) 271-6821. 310 St. Joseph Street, Suttons Bay, MI 49682. Marine accessories and supplies.

GLEN LAKE MARINA AND RESORT (616) 334-4556. M-72, Empire, MI 49630. Marine sales and service, parts and accessories. Boat rentals, sales, and slips. Waterskiing, wind surfing, sailing, and fishing.

MONSTREY'S GENERAL STORE AND SPORT SHOP. (616) 946-0018. 8332 Bingham Road, Traverse City, MI 49654. Boat rentals; pontoon boats, sailboards, small sailboats, fishing boats, and outboard motors.

THE HARBOR BOAT SHOP (616) 922-3020. 13240 S. West-Bayshore, Traverse City, MI 49654. Boat sales, ship's store, clothing, rain gear, boat shoes.

JON'S BARBER AND TACKLE SHOP (616) 271-3424. 119 St. Joseph, Suttons Bay, MI 49682. One unique shop for the sportsman. Jon's window alone is worth a trip to see, filled with lots of fishing memorabilia from the 1930s on. Besides atmosphere he offers complete fishing supplies, tackle, waders, boots, and fishing licenses.

Fishing and Boating

11

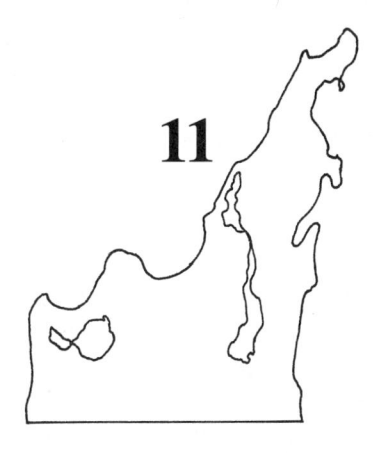

Seasons of Recreation

Whatever season she enters,
She enters it with grace.
Spring, summer, fall, winter—
She clothes them all in lace.

Leelanau is synonymous with recreation. Whatever outdoor activity, you'll probably find it here and enjoy it immensely! Swim in crystal-clear lakes, roam down pristine beaches, perhaps finding a Petoskey stone or two. Canoe a gentle river. Hike along miles of trails. Dive some of the best scuba sites in the state. Enjoy the area's four public golf courses. You'll experience some of the finest downhill and cross-country skiing, with endless trails.

Seasons of Recreation

BEACHES

Picture endless miles of sandy beach, intermingled with occasional rock-strewn points, and gentle surf that can suddenly turn into six-foot waves. For a true beach person, this combination spells hours of endless enjoyment—swimming, sailboarding, or walks down the shore. Off-season provides a feeling of isolation that's not isolation at all, if one is in tune with nature. Most beaches, if not all, provide a picnic area, rest rooms, and playground.

1. Empire Municipal Beach
2. Dunes Climb
3. Manitou Island
4. Glen Lake Picnic Area
5. Glen Haven Beach
6. D. H. Day Campground
7. Glen Arbor Municipal Beach
8. Old Settlers Park
9. Good Harbor Bay (Route 669)
10. Good Harbor Bay (Route 651)
11. Leland Municipal Beach
12. Leland Township Park
13. Peterson Park
14. Leelanau State Park
15. *Northport Municipal Beach
16. *Suttons Bay Municipal Beach
17. Centerville Township Park
18. *Elmwood Township Park

* Denotes lifeguard on duty. Otherwise swim at your own risk.

FALL COLOR TOURS

Seeing the Leelanau in any season is always appealing, but the fall colors really show off the county's hills and lakes. Late September

Seasons of Recreation

through October soon begin to come alive in a blaze of color as crimson sparks against the golds, yellows, and against pines, and other still-verdant greenery.

So comes the question, Where can we go for a color tour? Practically any road one embarks on in the Leelanau is beautiful, be it fall, summer, winter, or spring. The most popular route to travel is along M-22, a designated Lake Michigan Shoreline Scenic Circle

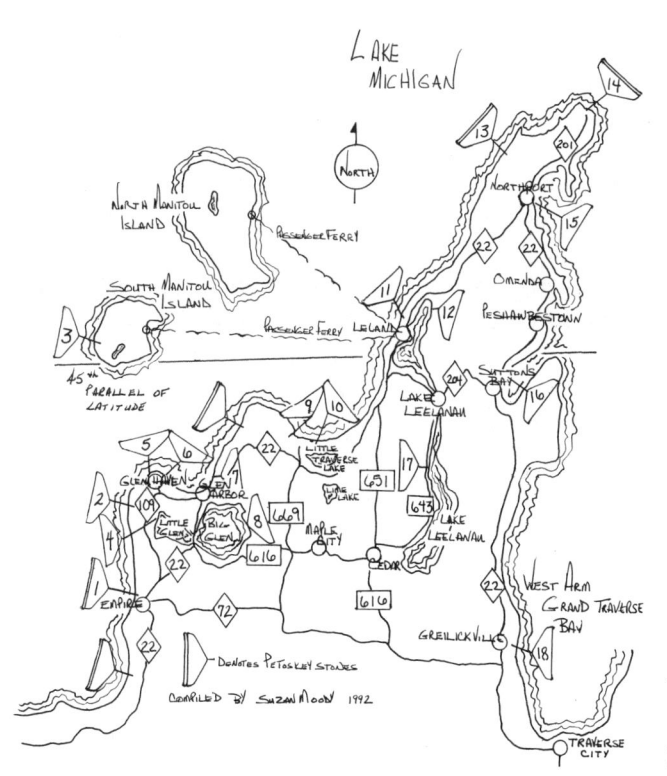

Tour. This route will lead you along the entire edge of the county. Definitely plan at least the entire day for this trip. Fill it with interesting stops in shops, museums, farm markets, wineries, and beaches.

If you start your tour in Traverse City, you'll travel to the village of Suttons Bay, next Omena, and Northport. At this point, you may want to travel nine miles north of Northport to the Grand Traverse Lighthouse. It's next to impossible to get lost, as there are signs leading the way out on this narrow jut, the tip of the peninsula. Heading back south some, you enter Leland and historic Fishtown, at the riverfront. South of Leland, the road on either side is forested with magnificent trees, gives glimpses of Lake Michigan, and has wonderfully elegant homes, coupled with quaint cottages and family farmsteads. You will pass Sugar Loaf Resort and the Homestead Resort, and enter into "Sleeping Bear Country" for the next thirty miles or so. When going through Glen Arbor, do not resist stopping in this artistic community. Turn left at the blinker light in Glen Arbor, still M-22, and in a few miles you will be crossing "the narrows." The scenery here is breathtaking! Farther on and you will be near the Dune Climb, part of the National Lakeshore. Then on to hospitable Empire, home of the Sleeping Bear Dunes National Lakeshore park headquarters and interpretive center. The route between the Dune Climb and Empire is especially pretty because of the road's gradual descent into the hills, with Lake Michigan looming to the west. Truly, all roads in the Leelanau lead to beautiful sights.

Another way to see the county is to go off the beaten path, so to speak. For detailed instructions, should you not want to map out your own out-of-the-way tour, write the Leelanau Peninsula Chamber of Commerce, P.O. Box 212, Lake Leelanau, MI 49653.

CAMPING

What better way to enjoy beautiful Leelanau than by experiencing

Seasons of Recreation

her as close to nature as possible? Your camping experience here is one you'll treasure for years, and you'll want to return again and again. Covered here are campgrounds on the mainland, including the National Lakeshore. Camping on the Manitou islands is covered in chapter 9. Rates are not covered here. It is suggested you call or write the facility of your choice for further information or a brochure or both.

NATIONAL PARK SERVICE CAMPGROUNDS (616) 326-5134. Sleeping Bear Dunes National Lakeshore, Box 277, Empire, MI 49634. D. H. Day Campground is located one and a half miles west of Glen Arbor, in a beautiful, heavily wooded area. There are a hundred rustic campsites available with vault toilets and sanitation disposal. No electric hookups.

Back country camping is permitted at the WHITE PINE CAMPGROUND along the Platte Plains Trail and at the VALLEY VIEW CAMPGROUND north of Glen Arbor (near the Homestead). North and South Manitou islands, accessible by ferry from Leland, also provide extensive backpacking and hiking opportunities.

LEELANAU STATE PARK (616) 386-5422. 15310 N. Lighthouse Point Road, Northport, MI 49670. At the very tip of the Leelanau peninsula, ten miles north of Northport. The park is within thirteen hundred acres, and offers fifty rustic sites, pit toilets, no electricity. There is a nice, large picnic area and playground. Also swimming, fishing, and eight and a half miles of trails for hiking—in winter a nice place for cross-country skiing. A state park motor vehicle permit is required.

LITTLE FINGER BEACH TRAVEL PARK (616) 256-7236. 3101 S. Lake Shore Drive, Lake Leelanu, MI 49653.. Three and a half miles south of the village of Lake Leelanau on South Lake Leelanau. There are shady or grassy sites available. Also offered: boat launch ramp, playground, boat and motor rentals, laundry facilities, and a little stream meandering through the grounds for children to fish or play in. Seasonal sites as well as docks are available. A wonderful plus to this campground is that they do not offer a recreation room for pinball and video machines. This leaves "children to enjoy nature as

137

Seasons of Recreation

camping was intended." They sell bait, ice cream, and firewood. There are 166 sites available, most with full hookup, twenty-five with water and electric.

SLEEPY BEAR CAMPGROUND (616) 326-5566. 6760 W. Empire Highway (M-72), Empire, MI 49630. A very pretty campground with all shady sites. There is a heated pool and modern rest rooms with showers. Nice playground. All hookups available; 132 sites.

THE HOMEWOOD (616) 386-5831. 415 North M-22, Northport, MI 49670. Just inside the village limits of Northport; the owners take pride in the grounds. Campsite rates are reasonable. Sites with or without electricity are available. It is just a short walk to a sandy beach, which has a lifeguard on duty. Also the marina and village shops and restaurants are within walking distance. Bathhouse with showers. Washers and dryers also on premises.

LEELANAU PINES CAMPGROUND (616) 228-5742. 6500 Leelanau Pines Drive, Cedar, MI 49621. Though the streets are paved, one still gets that "up north" feeling in this well-kept park. It is right on South Lake Leelanau with a beautiful, safe sandy beach area. Sites range from primitive and wooded to open grassy sites near the waterfront. It offers two very clean bathhouses, laundry facilities, grocery, as well as a boating dock ramp and even a trout stream within the park. There are 150 sites; 62 with sewer. Seasonal sites available.

LIME LAKE CAMPGROUND (616) 228-6251. 6354 Lime Lake Road, Cedar, MI 49621. Lime Lake is one of the prettiest small lakes you could ever find, and the name aptly fits it. This campground has thirty sites. Dump station.

WINDJAMMER (616) 946-7442. 11998 S. West Bayshore Drive, Traverse City, MI 49684. Two miles north of Traverse City on M-22. There are five full hookup sites as well as three tent sets. Use of two beaches on West Grand Traverse Bay and Cedar Lake and hot tub.

DOWNHILL SKIING

Skiing in the Leelanau is really special. Many of these slopes offer views offer rewarding views of Lake Michigan, the Manitous, and many small lakes as a panoramic backdrop. This coupled with the benefit of lake-effect snow makes quite a treat for the ski enthusiast.

Presently there are two ski resorts in Leelanau, Sugar Loaf and the Homestead.

SUGAR LOAF (616) 228-5461 or (800) 748-0117. (For lodging information see chapter 4.)

Sugar Loaf Resort is ablaze with activity year-round, and for the skier this is an especially exciting place. Starting in mid-December there is the "Shred-off" snow board competition: in midwinter come the United States Ski Association's Freestyle Competition and Mid-America Race Series—Slalom and Giant Slalom; the Junior NASTAR Open; the Special Olympics; and a host of other nationally and internationally scheduled events.

To complement the competition, Sugar Loaf Mountain has always provided the skier with five hundred vertical feet, including relaxing, mile-long Sugar and Spice to its ultimate challenge, Awful, Awful, the Midwest's steepest. Beginning in 1992, a totally new area called the "Manitou Extreme" was introduced. Two expert runs and two intermediate runs have been recontoured and transformed, resulting in the ultimate extreme—extreme length, extreme variety, extreme challenge, extreme racing, and extreme fun. This new area boasts the longest run in Michigan's Lower Peninsula, and also boasts a Federation of International Skiing (F.I S.) race hill—a rare find in the Midwest. The views are spectacular, overlooking the Manitou islands, the sand dunes, inland lakes, and rolling hills. Ski instruction and rentals available; full- and half-day lift tickets. Special packages also. For further information, contact Sugar Loaf Resort.

HOMESTEAD RESORT (616) 334-5000. M-22, Glen Arbor, MI 49636. This is a lovely place to ski, for it is right on Lake Michigan with extraordinary views. There are three lifts, one tow, and thirteen, which are lit for night skiing. Rentals and ski instruction are available. The Homestead is open for skiing on Friday through Sunday until 9 p.m. and daily December 26 through January 1.

CROSS-COUNTRY SKIING

Many popular ski trails will keep a cross-country skier busy; a variety of terrain choices and scenery are unmatched anywhere. You may choose many of the lakeshore's summer hiking trails, which double as cross-country trails in winter. There is a charge for a ski pass. Ski instruction available both in regular and telemark cross-country.

SUGAR LOAF (616) 228-5461 or (800) 748-0117. 4500 Sugar Loaf Mountain Road, Cedar, MI 49621. Twenty-six kilometers of groomed and track-set trails wind through some of northern Michigan's most scenic countryside. The trails also access the Sleeping Bear Dunes National Lakeshore's fifty-kilometer trail system. There are guided backcountry tours and cross-country and telemark lessons.

1. Extra Sweet, 2.4 km (easy). A trail with several long gradual hills that make it attractive for all skiers. The trail winds along the golf course fairways with good wind protection and varied scenery.

2. Grand Boulevard, 4.2 km (easy). This trail is two-way its entire length. It connects with Sugar Bowl Trail; together they form the core of the trail system. The return leg is a gradual, long climb, broken by several level stretches to break up the climb and add interest.

3. Peppi's Bench, 2.8 km (more difficult "plus" trail). Midway down the Grand Boulevard Trail Peppi's Bench takes off! They rejoin at a lower elevation. The trail winds down a "bench" area about two-thirds of the way down along the north side of Sugar Loaf. Some spectacular views of Lake Michigan, Little Traverse Lake, and Pyramid Point. Expect some exciting dips and bends before a final, downhill run to the lower elevation.

4. Sugar Bowl, 3.0 km (more difficult). Sugar Bowl is joined either at the bottom of Twister or the end of Grand Boulevard. The terrain is well within the capabilities of most skiers, other than one fairly steep hill. The trail winds its way back and forth within the confines of a west-facing "bowl." There are substantial level stretches and a good number of hills of varying length and grade. The "bowl" is entirely wooded.

5. Bowl Over, 1.0 km (most difficult). This run contains several steep, fast downhills and a short, steep uphill climb. This short, challenging "bubble" adds an exciting variation for the advanced skier.

6. Twister, 3.0 km (most difficult). Said to ski "like a cyclone," this trail provides one of the most exciting cross-country downhills that can be found anywhere. After a short climb at the beginning of the trailhead, it dips and rushes down and across a long slope for over a mile. At this point, you can cross over to Sugar Bowl or take a long but interesting climb back up the Twister (with two short two-way sections), either for another descent, to reach the Double Dipper, or return to the resort.

7. Double Dipper, 4.0 km (more difficult "plus" trails). This trail traverses the upper reaches of a heavily wooded west slope. The trail offers several quick, exciting down-and-ups with an S turn. Next, a long, fast, open field downhill with lovely views over Lime Lake and Leelanau's rugged hills. After the field, there are several fun downhills, then the trail crosses a small stream and begins a gradual climb that traverses back to the start.

8. Cherry Pie, 2.5 km (easiest). An excellent choice for the beginning skier. This is a mostly level trail that winds through a nearby orchard.

HOMESTEAD RESORT offers 36 km of groomed and tracked cross-country trails that access the National Park System's Bay View Trail (see below).

SLEEPING BEAR DUNES NATIONAL LAKESHORE (616) 326-5134. Because of the danger of avalanche in winter, not all hiking trails are advisable for use during winter. Following is a list and short description of the trails that the park recommends. Trail maps available at no charge to skiers. The park has mapped and marked about forty miles of trails. They are laid out in such a way as to take advantage of the terrain, providing the shortest uphill climbs and the longest downhill runs. Trail conditions vary from day to day. Heavy weekend use and alternate daytime thawing/nighttime freezing will turn even the most easy, gentle slopes into icy fast advanced hills. Be aware of snow conditions.

 1. OLD INDIAN TRAIL. This 3.45-mile trail is divided into an easy loop and an advanced loop. It traverses a pine-hardwood forest with one lookout on Lake Michigan.

 2. PLATTE PLAINS TRAIL. There are two trailheads serving this fourteen-mile trail. The trail is divided into several loops, the shortest about four miles. Most of the trail is easy skiing; there is one intermediate section and one advanced section. Vegetation is primarily pine-oak forest mingled with wetlands, open fields, and beech-maple forest. There are two scenic lookouts over Lake Michigan.

 3. EMPIRE BLUFF TRAIL. This is a mile-a-half trail, round-trip. There are two spectacular overlooks. Vegetation is beech-maple forest with a few fields interspersed.

 4. WINDY MORAINE TRAIL. This is a one-and-a-half-mile advanced trail through woods and trail. There is a scenic overlook of Glen Lake and the Sleeping Bear Dunes.

 5. SCENIC DRIVE TRAIL. A ten-mile trail of easy and intermediate skiing with one .6-mile advanced run. The trail follows unplowed Pierce Stocking Scenic Drive. The two-mile Shauger Hill hiking trail is also part of this system. There are four scenic lookouts. A camera is advised.

 6. ALLIGATOR HILL TRAIL. This comprises 8.6 miles of trail divided into an easy, intermediate, and advanced loop. The vegetation is mostly hardwood forest with some open fields. There are two scenic lookouts with views over Lake Michigan and Glen Lake. This seems to be everyone's favorite.

 7. BAY VIEW TRAIL. This trail is ten miles of mixed easy and intermediate skiing, and two short advanced sections. Two trailheads serve this system, one at the Homestead Resort and one on Thorson Road. Terrain varies between beech-maple forest to open farm country. Lookout Point offers a view of Lake Michigan and the beautiful

countryside.

The Homestead Resort grooms this trail under a concession contract with the National Park Service. Grooming takes place on Fridays, Saturdays, Sundays, and holidays. There is a fee; pay at the Homestead Resort ticket office.

8. GOOD HARBOR BAY TRAIL. This is a 2.8-mile easy loop through pine and hardwood; one section is through the dunes near Lake Michigan.

This 1.5-mile trail is classified for advanced skiers. Several hilly sections traverse a hardwood forest interspersed with meadows. The trail ends on top of Empire bluff with a view overlooking Lake Michigan and the village of Empire.

LEELANAU STATE PARK. There are eight and a half miles of cross-county trails to explore two miles north of Northport next to the Clinton Woosley Airport. The terrain is beautifully wooded and slighly rolling. Enough downhill runs will keep the intermediate skier happy. The trail passes a small lake and offers access to Cathead Bay (Lake Michigan). It's a favorite trail for many.

GOLFING

SUGAR LOAF VILLAGE (616) 228-5461. Sugar Loaf Mountain Road, Cedar, MI 49621. Said to be a golfer's paradise, it presently has the area's longest courses: 6,901 yards from the championship tees. An additional eighteen-hole golf course is being designed. Host to the Celebrity Classic Golf Tournament.

DUNES GOLF CLUB (616) 326-5390. M-72, Empire, MI 49670. Seventeen miles west of Traverse City. This is a challenging 3,277-yard course, which plays to a par 35.

MATHESON GREENS (616) 386-5171. Matheson Road at Swede Road, Northport, MI 49670. A very beautiful and challenging golf course. It boasts 6,416 yards, par 72, and offers eighteen championship holes. It has been designed to challenge the expert yet not intimidate the novice. There is a pro shop, driving range, and restaurant. Power carts and club rental.

VERONICA VALLEY (616) 256-9449. 4341 S. Lake Leelanau Drive (County Road 641), Lake Leelanau, MI 49653. Built in 1991, Veronica Valley is as pretty and scenic as its name. The course was carved out of ninety-three beautiful acres set in a green valley with shimmering ponds, and surrounded by tree-covered hills. The course has nine holes, featuring a challenging 3,203-yard, par 35. They have golf supplies, rental clubs, power and pull carts, snacks, and soft drinks.

DIVING—MANITOU PASSAGE STATE UNDERWATER PRESERVE

The Manitou Passage State Underwater preserve comprises 282 square miles of fresh water, which surround over a hundred locations containing shipwrecks, historic sights, and unique geologic features. It is headed up by the Manitou Preserve Committee and the Northwest Michigan Maritime Museum. There are plans to locate a museum in a building in Empire.

The cool fresh waters of Lake Michigan and the other Great Lakes have preserved much of what has come to lie beneath them. The State of Michigan passed legislation in 1980, largely supported by Michigan sport divers, ensuring that this sport will remain a high-quality activity. Stiffer penalties for abuse were enacted in 1988.

The Manitou Preserve offers a great diversity, from historic dock ruins to fascinating shipwrecks of two centuries ago. Visibility in the preserve is from twelve to twenty-five feet.

The most popular dive site is the *Francisco Morazan,* which ran aground in November 1960. It lies in only fifteen feet of water, making for an easy dive for the beginner. The hull, 246-feet in length, still contains some machinery in the engine room. Much of this wreck is not submerged, but divers are discouraged from trying to explore the structure above water level.

A few hundred yards south of the *Francisco Morazan* lies a wooden steamer, the *Walter L. Frost,* which ran aground in 1905. Divers enjoy this wreck because so much remains of this old vessel. There are large sections of the hull, machinery, boilers, and other related artifacts for the diver to explore.

Divers can also explore dock ruins throughout the area. These massive pilings were driven into the sandy bottom of the lake to create docks for the steamers in the 1800s for the loading of fruit, lumber, grain, and other products. The dock ruins are sites for many interesting artifacts, including anchors and broken pieces from the many shipwrecks that occurred here.

For local diving information contact: SCUBA NORTH (616) 947-2520. 13380 S. West-Bayshore Drive, Traverse City, MI 49684. Scuba North is a full-service dive shop, with air, instruction, rentals, equipment, and charters.

CANOEING

Canoe down the scenic and gentle Crystal River, viewing nature as the early Indians viewed it, silently paddling the river. . . . The shores are state-owned on either side of the Crystal. You will find the area uninhabited and full of wildlife busy in natural surroundings. Plan on a two-and-a-half-hour trip. Three miles from the Sleeping Bear Dunes National Park.

CRYSTAL RIVER CANOE LIVERY (616) 334-3090 or 3831. On M-22 at the Glen Arbor Shell station. Canoe and kayak rentals. Group rates available. Open 9 a.m. to 5 p.m.

HIKING

There are twelve hiking trails in the Sleeping Bear Dunes National Park. All trails are marked and maintained by the park. Each trailhead

Seasons of Recreation

has a parking area and a map box containing detailed trail maps. There are also trails on North and South Manitou islands, and in the Leelanau State Park, which has 8½ miles of trails. Please stay on designated trails to help prevent erosion and damage to vegetation. Off-trail hikers can quickly produce paths that take years to revegetate. If you venture cross-country, take a compass and topographic map and avoid private property. Take care to avoid disturbing plants and animals; threatened and endangered species occur throughout the area.

    1. OLD INDIAN. Two loops, 2.3 and 2.25 miles in length. These short loops lead through flat or gently rolling wooded terrain of mixed hardwood and pines. A portion of this trail follows an old Indian pathway to the beach. Excellent view.

    2. PLATTE PLAINS. This trail consists of a series of loops, each three to six miles long. The total trail length is fifteen miles. Mostly flat terrain, some rolling hills, and some short steep hills that lead to the White Pine Back-country Campground.

    3. EMPIRE BLUFF NATURE TRAIL. This hike is one and a half miles round-trip. The terrain is hilly and leads to a very scenic viewpoint, four hundred feet above Lake Michigan. At this overlook, you can survey much of the lakeshore. The Sleeping Bear Dune, which gave its name to the entire dune complex, appears as a small dark hill on top of the high sandy bluff. Wind erosion has destroyed much of this historic dune, which was a landmark for travelers on Lake Michigan.

    4. WINDY MORAINE. A one-and-a-half-mile loop through hilly terrain in a beech-maple forest, old farm fields, and a pine plantation. This trail has numbered points of interest, to show the importance of nature's diversity. From a high point along the trail, you'll view Glen Lake, Lake Michigan, and the Sleeping Bear Dunes.

    5. SHAUGER HILL. A 2.4-mile loop through a beech-maple forest with hilly terrain. There are a few small clearings and a pine plantation.

    6. COTTONWOOD TRAIL. A one-and-a-half-mile trek through moderately rolling dunes. Part of this trail is through loose sands. Vegetation is low, consisting of grasses, shrubs, and wildflowers.

    7. THE DUNES TRAIL-SLEEPING BEAR POINT TRAIL. A three-mile round-trip trail through strenuous, sandy dunes. Allow three

to four hours. The terrain is steep and rugged with grasses, shrubs, and wildflowers.

8. THE DUNES (Sleeping Bear Point). A 2.8-mile loop through moderately rolling dunes. A short spur near the beginning of the trail leads out to Lake Michigan. This trail can be strenuous, for much of it is through loose sand.

9. ALLIGATOR HILL. Composed of three loops through hill terrain, two and a half to three miles each, plus a spur trail of .8 mile, off the first loop. Vegetation consists of beech-maple forest, brushy fields, and a pine plantation. There is a view of Lake Michigan along the first loop and a view of Glen Lake at the end of the spur trail. Both views are somewhat obscured by trees.

10. BAY VIEW. Nine miles of hilly trail, divided into several shorter loops. Your hike will take you through beech-maple forest and a pine plantation. Lookout Point gives a beautiful view of Lake Michigan and the surrounding countryside.

11. PYRAMID POINT. A hilly, 2.4-mile trail through beech-maple forest, open fields, and sand dunes. This trail leads to a high panoramic view of Lake Michigan half a mile from the trailhead. This is also a popular launch site for hang gliders.

12. GOOD HARBOR BAY. A 2.8-mile flat, nearly square loop. The trail passes through some dunes near the start and then enters a forested zone. You will pass through some wetlands in the low areas between the ridges.

LEELANAU STATE PARK. About two miles north of the village of Northport next to Clinton Woolsey Airport. Eight miles of trails in a wooded and rolling setting. Part of the trail winds through a wetland area next to a small lake.

LEELANAU SCENIC RAILROAD

To see Leelanau County from a different perspective, take a ride on the Leelanau Scenic Railroad. Leave behind the hustle and bustle of traffic and ride through the fragrant backwoods, meadows full of beautiful wildflowers, lovely orchards, and cornfields. You will be surprised at the different sights. The whistle toots at every intersection and people wave from their cars and backyards. The lullaby clickity-clack of the ties will rock you into a trip back in time. Most people agree that the trip is very relaxing.

The Leelanau Scenic Railroad was in the making for over five years. Its maiden run was August 3, 1991. The train is composed of a powerful diesel engine, passenger cars from the Reading Railroad back east, and a wonderful caboose, complete with potbellied stove. The railroad is undergoing restoration. A steam engine and more passenger cars are proposed for the future.

The railroad runs between Traverse City (Grelickville) and Suttons Bay; trains depart twice daily from each point. To find the Traverse City depot, take S. West-Bayshore Drive (M-22), about two miles north of E. Traverse Highway (M-72). Look for the bright red Leelanau Scenic Railroad sign on your left, opposite Elmwood Township Park. Phone (616) 947-6667 for further information and departure schedule.

SEASONS OF FESTIVALS

What better way to celebrate being in Leelanau than with its tempo of festivities? Listed here are some of the most well known: *January through March:* Lots of excitement at Sugar Loaf Resort. *May:* Spring Nature Festival, Suttons Bay. *June:* Wine Festival, Leland; Classic Boat Show, Suttons Bay. *July:* Polka Festival, Cedar; Harbor Days festival, Art Fair and Music in the Park, Northport; Open Water Swim Challenge; Leland; Arts and Crafts Fair, Lake Leelanau; Suttons Bay; Street Dance, Maple City. *August:* Art Festival, Suttons Bay; Leelanau Wine Festival, Music in the Park, and Labor Day Fish Boil, Northport. *September:* Grand Traverse Bay Offshore Classics Festivities, Northport. *October:* Arts and Crafts Festival, Cedar; Northport Fall Festival; Suttons Bay Fall Festival.

12

Seasonal Reflections and Promises

Reflections and promises—
Each one will have its own,
For none can enter her
And for long stay unbeknown.

To try to capture a sense of the heart of the Leelanau, this chapter was created. Who but its residents could tell their impressions, experiences, and knowledge in relation to the land and the water of the Leelanau? The only criteria given to each one were: Think of your seasonal reflections. Think of what you would promise to Leelanau if she could hear (and she does, through these pages). Also: Speak from the heart and, most important, can you do it? Not all persons can place themselves so deeply into a given area that they could understand what this chapter meant to accomplish.

The Leelanau is a very special place to many special people. It was wished that many more could have been included in this chapter. An entire book could be written about just them. The ones included

Seasonal Reflections and Promises

here somehow naturally fell into place, and at the right time—as if they belonged in this chapter. They instinctively knew what was meant to be said from their hearts.

The Leelanau Twelve

Mollie Weeks
Owner of The Cottage Book Shop of Glen Arbor.

Beauty and tranquility seem to me to be the essence of Leelanau County. There is such diversity, from wide Lake Michigan beaches and dunes to the hundreds of acres of orchards and vineyards, to steep, forested hills and the many small lakes scattered throughout the county.

The changes of the seasons are also an important ingredient of the pleasure of living or visiting here, and multiply the beauty to be enjoyed. The unique environment has also been an inspiration for poets, essayists, novelists, historians, photographers, and the many artists living and flourishing here.

The motto of Michigan is: If you seek a pleasant peninsula, look about you. If you seek beauty, tranquility, and creativity, look about the Leelanau peninsula.

Dennis Stanford
Leelanau County's country vet, who owns All Creatures Great & Small, a veterinary house call practice.

In early spring, after the ice goes off the inland lakes, I walk out slowly into the water and the cold envelops me. The air is heavy with the scent of the pines. Green leaves and white blossoms of the trillium push up through the damp earth.

As summer approaches, the rolling hills become alive with a tapestry of color, as cherry, apple, pear, peach, and apricot trees each bloom in order, and the earth sways with the towering golden stalks of wheat.

The crystalline sheen of ice has left the lakes now to be replaced by a phosphorescent shimmering of light under the full moons of summer, when the only sounds are the lapping of water as waves race along the shoreline of Lake Michigan.

Then the leaves of the hardwoods will reflect every color of the rainbow and just as quickly blanket the ground to become the mulch of next year's life.

And on to the still of the winter, blanketed by snow that silences all but the screech and the rustle of wings of the owl.

Every season holds me in wonder as I travel the back roads of Leelanau County, a place that is so much like the best of every other place all in one.

Julia Dickinson
Former teacher, historian, and writes the Glen Arbor news for the *Leelanau Enterprise*. With her husband, Fred, and daughter, Grace, both noted photographers, they run Dickinson Galleries in Glen Arbor.

Reflections of Leelanau span the years from 1914 to the present. Those were the days when boats came to the Glen Haven dock bringing Chicagoans for a weekend of fresh air, fishing in the lakes and streams, and relaxing in the sunshine along the shore.

It was the time when children built rafts for high adventures in the shallow water, played with neighborhood boys and girls, and found bits of wood embedded in the sand—remnants of the lumbering days.

Reflections also come from East Leland, where kerosene lamps provided light in the evenings, when wood shutters were dropped when the rain came, when hand pumps brought water for the kitchen, and when food was cooked on wood stoves.

The reflections we have are also of quiet times of hiking in the woods, of tasting Michigan cherries for the first time.

And promises. We want to keep this beautiful land as unspoiled as possible, recognizing at the same time that changes are occurring every day. We must share the lakeshores and the highways and the woodlands. We must preserve and protect the land. We must adjust to the new and different philosophies of enjoyment. And we must record the past memories and recollections for the generations to come.

Thomas M. Kelly

Marine biologist and consultant, Executive Director of the Inland Seas Education Association, and owns *Cygnet* Sailing Expeditions.

Leelanau is a special place for me because of the water. We are everywhere close to water: marshes and bogs, constant-cold streams, lakes, and Lake Michigan and Grand Traverse Bay. Even the hills and valleys that give the county its character and climate were shaped by water (frozen water, that is, and the glacial meltwater that followed).

Being almost surrounded by water makes for a pleasant isolation. You can only get here on purpose. We are not on the way to any other place. Unless you are traveling by boat, the water is a connecting medium. It appeals to me that we are connected nautically with Boston, Bombay, and Buenos Aires. There is a freedom in knowing that our horizon is not confined by an inland lake, and with the right boat you could sail away to. . . . There is something special here about the people. I don't know if it is the landscape, the waters, or the climate that makes it this way. I only know that there are a lot of unique people in Leelanau. Some have family names that have been here for over a hundred years. Some have just moved here. But these are a friendly, creative, preserving folk, and I am proud to be among them.

Kevin Herman
Fourth-generation cherry farmer.

To me, Leelanau County means changes. These changes are inevitable. I remember my father telling me there was lake frontage just north of Leland that sold for a hundred dollars a lot. The funny thing was you could have bought a whole mile. Back in the fifties, lake frontage didn't mean that much to people. It was only minimally productive as farmland with tendencies of rough terrain. Boating was the transportation of supplies. Pleasure boating and sailing were not prevalent. I've been told that cargo boats were common on the lakes.

Transportation has changed a lot in the county. Visitors in our area many times get bewildered as they travel the winding road systems. The two main reasons for these unstructured routes were the many lakes and the horse and buggy. Many of the roads in Leelanau County are old horse trails. Many trains used to travel in the county. The train hauled wood from some of the local mills. In the winter the local people would have work bees to shovel a path through the deep snow so the train could get through.

Farming in Leelanau County has changed; most of the farmers were general farmers producing only enough to provide for themselves. The main crop was potatoes. Today, because of the special climate that the Great Lakes provides, the main crop is cherries. As a fourth-generation cherry farmer, whose grandfather worked the ground with a team of horses, I appreciate motorized equipment. Farms of the past were smaller because of the manual labor required. Cherries were hand-harvested with ladder, pails, and lugs. Large crews were needed each summer for the harvest, and they came from all over. I remember hauling lugs of cherries to the processor. The lugs were swung by hand into the air over a pool of water; another person would have to catch the empty lug before it hit the water. Today, shakers, catching frames, forklifts, and stake trucks simplify the harvest; few laborers are required. In a farming community, the villages were quiet during the summer months. Because everyone was in the field working, little time was left for commerce. Many farmers were poor—all their money was tied into the crop, anticipating the harvest. As I reflect, I miss the sense of community between farmers, families, and neighbors. I miss the "gathered" community working together to hand-plant trees, build barns, and harvest—activities much like the present-day church socials and community festivals.

Beverly Gillmore
She transformed her life when she decided for health reasons to leave New York City as a journalist and move to the Leelanau.

A snowy owl and two coyote pups on the Sleeping Bear Dune. . . a bald eagle soaring by. . . . As a realist who spent twenty-three years as a journalist in New York City, I marveled at a lunar eclipse started over the Glen Lake Narrows one recent summer. Driving home at twilight through Cedar two years ago, I observed a wolf loping across a wintry field. I was awestruck by the night rainbow that stretched from Pyramid Point on Lake Michigan to the eastern horizon during a northern lights display in November 1991. The rainbow was framed on shimmering walls of red, violet, pink, green, and white light.

If you are fortunate enough to live here or spend part of your year up north, you know about the healing properties of clean air and water. When the Ice Age glacier retreated ten thousand years ago, it left a natural "field of dreams." Since then, the smart people have come to the Leelanau peninsula!

Owen Bahle
Great-grandson of Lars Esten Bahle, who founded Bahle's of Suttons Bay in 1876. The Bahle family continues the tradition.

I have witnessed teams of horses tied to hitching posts in front of my father's store (Bahle's) alongside automobiles. I saw a team become alarmed and move into the plate glass window of the co-op store with no injury. As kids we spent a lot of time watching Loren Walters, the self-taught blacksmith, shoe horses and repair wagons. We enjoyed self-taught swimming off the company docks. The lifestyle in the 1920s in Leelanau County was definitely rural; tourism was not to develop until later.

Potatoes were the early major crop in Leelanau County, to be replaced by cherries along with the importance of tourism. The depression of the 1930s was real, but we all seemed to adjust so that we didn't feel too deprived. The slow economy continued into the 1940s and 1950s while the rest of the country was thriving. The great industrial growth in the cities caused by the demands of World War II did not affect this area very much. There was a long period when many of the younger generation left for the opportunities of the city. My wife and I really felt a bit alone in our age-group in the mid-1940s.

I am especially appreciative that I was able to grow up in Suttons Bay. It has been a wonderful experience.

Pete Edwards
Director of Marketing and Public Relations, Sugar Loaf Resort.

Almost by accident I came to Leelanau County over ten years ago, but it was no accident that I stayed. I flew in to interview for a position that sounded exactly like what I was looking for—working with kids and coaching. The interview lasted several days and gave me the opportunity to canoe the Crystal River, hike the trails on Alligator Hill, run the dirt roads on Miller Hill, and see the wonderful things the county offers. What a great setting for working with kids! What a great chance to expose them to building appreciation for Leelanau County's natural beauty and the need to preserve and protect the environment!Today my wife, Lissa, and I share the beauty and resources of the county with our own children. Every season is special to us, and the activities are always many and varied. Each spring brings the thrill of the mushroom hunt (morelling) and an excuse to hike together for miles almost every day after work. The summer is ideal for paddling the old canoe in the Crystal, in smaller lakes, and in our favorite beaver pond, with time out for picking wild berries along the way. The fall colors and the salmon run are always great, regardless of the weather. Come winter, Leelanau County's cross-country and downhill skiing lure us outside for more family activity together.

Every season is special in Leelanau, and the outdoor activities are endless. Thanks to the dedicated farmers, who have maintained the county's agricultural areas, and to the National Lakeshore for preserving miles of beach, forest, and field. The county is an oasis, an area rich with natural beauty. All the time it has a unique coziness that makes Leelanau—the county and peninsula—an area to love and explore no matter the season, no matter your background, and no matter what kind of car you drive.

Peggy N. Core
A Leelanau native and artiste extraordinaire, Peggy owns Pweavings Plus, her gallery of work at L. Mawby Vineyards.

Each artist's work is a reflection of physical surroundings and emotional experiences, transformed tactually through a specific medium. Leelanau County's water-spattered, rolling drumlins dotted with hardwoods and evergreens continue to be my mirror of inspiration. . . at times

> *quiet as winter snow*
> *angry as spring lightning*
> *playful as summer blossoms*
> *restless as autumn leaves*
> *reflective as winter ice.*

Ice. . . icy winter whites move through grays and muddy browns, give way to bright greens and yellows, oranges, reds, violets, and purples, returning finally to cold blues, grays, and icy whites. Another year has come and gone, each a reflection of the one past.

Perhaps Leelanau County's Maker paused after the labor and said, "I make what I like, I like what I make." And it was as near a perfect reflection as the Maker could ever want.

Brian Price
Executive Director of the Leelanau Conservancy.

The Leelanau peninsula has a different "feel" and visual quality. We are all attracted to the variety and blend of landscape forms: forested hills grading into pocketed cedar swamps, hillside farms, high dunes, ancient shorelines, the miles of sandy beaches, and the way these elements combine to create the larger whole.

But unlike some other beautiful areas—the mountains and canyon lands and their remote beauty come to mind—our landscape invites participation and rewards each participant with a unique set of discoveries. In my work with the Leelanau Conservancy, every day I come across people who describe their special places. These destinations are usually scattered across the county and visited in much the same way that a trapper works a trap line: follow a circuit to see what nature reveals. A place to watch sunsets, a place to view storms rushing onshore, a place to hunt morels, to find lady's slippers in June, to go for an autumn hike.

Aldo Leopold noted that "the first principle of intelligent tinkering is to save all the pieces." Leelanau is a place of beauty and a place for people. We need to learn that the beauty is beyond our powers of creation. We can only see that future generations are afforded the opportunity to discover their own "special places."

David Taghon
President of the Village of Empire, and President of Empire Heritage Group.

Seasonal Reflections and Promises

Is there a more beautiful spot on the earth than Leelanau County? It's possible, but I doubt it. This beautiful peninsula seems to have it all. I appreciate living here more day by day. Sure, I make my living here, but much more than that, I soak in life here. I was born in Empire and here I shall remain, for I can think of no other area that fits me so well. I love the history here, as brief as it has been.

I love the people here because we share the common goals of either making a living here or making a life here after retirement. I make a point of touring the county many times each year, to visit each unique community and to share with them their challenges, changes, and accomplishments. Leelanau County has been entrusted to us to preserve for future generations, and I am glad to be part of this undertaking. The beautiful Lake Michigan sunsets, the peaceful rolling dunes, the reflections over beaver ponds, the changing seasons, and much more make Leelanau one of a kind.

Susan Jay Nichols
Proprietor of Fountain Point Resort.

I have been coming to Leelanau since I was three years old. I feel fortunate to have experienced living and working here. My fondest memories are of the special people who come to Fountain Point. Together, we have shared the music, polka dances, warm moonlit nights, s'mores on the beach, sunburns, the dune rides, maple sugar candy you could buy at Glen Haven, Steffens Fishery, and the way the Leland harbor used to be.

A lot of things aren't here anymore, and a lot of things have changed. But here I am a kid again; time has stood still. Over the years, I have lived in faraway places but my heart has always longed for the "blue of the water, the blue of the sky, and the cry of the gulls as they circle on high, Leelanau, Leelanau, Land of Delight."

Appendix

D.N.R. Access Sites

Site	Location	Ramp Code	Toilets	Parking Sites
W. Grand Traverse Bay	3 miles NE of Bingham Road.	2	yes	36
W. Lake Leelanau	6 miles NE of Cedar	3	yes	5
E. Lake Leelanau	1 mile W of Bingham	2	yes	20
S. Lake Leelanau	1 mile NW of Lake Leelanau	4	yes	10
N. Lake Leelanau	2 miles NE of Leland	2	yes	8
The Narrows (on L.Leelanau)	Lake Leelanau	1	yes	28
Carp River** (L. Leelanau access)	Leland	1	no	6

Appendix

Site	Location	Ramp Code	Toilets	Parking Sites
Cedar Lake	2 miles NW of Traverse City	3	yes	15
Glen Lake	5 miles NE of Empire	2	yes	20
Lime Lake	2 miles N of Maple City	2	yes	6
Armstrong Lake	5 miles SW of Maple City	3	yes	3
Solon Township** Park Cedar River (S. L. Leelanau access)	1 miles E of Cedar	2	no	8

*RAMP CODE
1. Hardsurfaced ramp with sufficient water depth to accommodate most trailerable boats.
2. A hard surfaced ramp, in areas of limited water depth, where launching and retrieving of larger boats may be difficult.
3. A gravely surfaced ramp.

**Special rules and regulations apply; special closing hours, rules against consumption of alcoholic beverages, or others. Also, this designates that site rules are established by an agency other then the D.N.R.

National Register Sites for Leelanau County

Bingham Township

Historic site name: Bingham District No. 5 Schoolhouse
Common site name: Bingham School District No. 1 Schoolhouse
Address: Southeast corner of Bingham Road (County Road 618) and County Road 633
Date listed: July 31, 1991

Glen Arbor Township

Historic site name: Glen Haven Village Historic District
Address: M-209
Date listed: June 24, 1983

Historic site naae: Hutzler's Barn
Address: North of cemetery
Date listed: January 3, 1978

Historic site name: Sleeping Bear Inn
Common site name: Glen Haven Inn
Address: M-209
Date listed: September 6 1979

Historic site name: Sleeping Bear Point Life-Saving Station
Common site name: Glen Haven Coast Guard Station
Address: North of Glen Haven, Sleeping Bear Dunes National Lakeshore
Date listed: April 26, 1979

Historic site name: South Manitou Island Lighthouse Complex and Life-Saving Station Historic District
Common site name: South Manitou Island Historic District
Address: Sandy Point
Date listed :   October 28, 1983

Leelanau Township

Historic site name: Grand Traverse Light Station
Common site name: Cathead Point
Address: North point of Leelanau peninsula, at the end of County Road 62 9
Date listed :   July 19, 1984

Historic site name: Grove Hill New Mission Church
Common site name: Omena Presbyterian Church
Address   M-22
Date listed: June 29, 1972

Appendix

Leland Township

Historic site name: Leland Historic District
Common site name: Fishtown
Address: Roughly bounded by the park, Main Street, Avenue A, and the harbor
Date listed: November 20, 1975

State Register Sites for Leelanau County

Bingham Township

Historic site name: Bingham District No. 5 Schoolhouse
Common site name: Bingham School District No. 1 Schoolhouse
Address: Southeast corner of Bingham Road (County Road 6183 and County Road 633
Date listed: October 23, 1987

Elmwood Township

Historic site name: Greilickville
Address: 129 S. West Bay Shore Drive
Date listed: November 27, 1972

Empire Village

Historic site name: Empire Lumber Company
Address: Village Park, Niagra Street
Date listed: November 7, 1977

Glen Arbor Township

Address: Sleeping Bear Dunes National Lakeshore, four miles west of Glen Arbor
Date listed: September 17, 1957

Historic site name: Frank E. Fisher Store
Common site name: Laird's Store

Registers of Historic Sites

Address: 5504 Southwest Manitou Trail (M-22)
Date listed: June 15, 1984

Historic site name: Glen Arbor Roller Mills
Address: 5402 Southwest Manitou Trail (M-22)
Date listed: November 7, 1977

Historic site name: South Manitou Island Lighthouse Complex and Life-Saving Station Historic District
Common site name: South Manitou Island Historic District
Address: Sandy Point
Date listed: September 21, 1976

Historic site name: Sylvan Inn
Address: M-109, just west of M-22 (Ray Street)
Date listed: August 15, 1975

Historic site name: Grand Traverse Light Station
Common site name: Cathead Point
Address: North point of Leelanau peninsula, at the end of County Road 629

Historic site name: Grove Hill New Mission Church
Common site name: Omena Presbyterian Church
Address: M-22
Date listed: October 29, 1971

Historic site name: Saint Wenceslaus Roman Catholic Church and Cemetery
Address: County Road 626 (Kolarik Road) at County Road 637
Date listed: July 20, 1989

Historic site name: Sunset Lodge
Address: Omena Point Road
Date listed: October 23, 1987

Historic site name: Woodhow Lodge
Address: County Road 629 (Lighthouse Point Road), east of Purkiss Road
Date listed: March 22, 1983

163

Appendix

Leland Township

Historic site name: Greycote
Common site name: Eleanor A. Hendrickson Cottage
Address: Northeast corner of Pearl and Lake Streets
Date listed: July 26, 1974

Historic site name: Leelanau County Jail
Address: 107 Chandler Street
Date listed: July 26, 1974

Historic site name: Leland Historic District
Common site name: Fishtown
Address: Roughly bounded by the park, Main Street, Avenue A, and the harbor
Date listed: June 28, 1973
Historic site name: Provemont General Store
Address: 102 Meinard Street
Date listed: June 20, 1991

Historic site name: Walter T. Best Women's Club House
Common site name: Leelanau Summer Art School
Address: Northeast corner of Main and Cedar streets
Date listed: July 20, 1989

Historic site name: W. K. Hatt Cottage
Common site name: Hatt's Hideout
Address: 410 N. Main Street
Date listed: April 19, 1990

Northport Village

Address: Village Marina, 105 Rose Street
Date listed: May 8, 1984

Historic site name: Howard E. Gill Building
Common site name: The Pier Group
Address: 206 N. Rose Street
Date listed: July 26, 1978

Registers of Historic Sites

Solon Township

Historic Site name: Manistee and Northeastern Railroad Cedar Depot
Common site name: Cedar Railroad Depot
Address: Sullivan Street and Railroad Avenue
Date listed: August 24, 1984

Suttons Bay Township

Historic site name: Fountain Point
Address: 990 South Lake Leelanau Drive (County Road 641)
Date listed: August 15, 1975

Appendix

References

In preparing this book I found the following printed materials helpful. I also compiled much information from various shop and resort brochures and from the chambers of commerce of Glen Arbor, Northport, Empire, Leland, and the Leelanau Peninsula Chamber of Commerce.

Blackbird, Andrew J. *History of the Chippewa and Ottawa Indians of Michigan, aGrammar of Their Language and Personal History of the Author.* 1887.

Clifton, J., G. Cornell, and J. McCluken. *People of the Three Fires.* Grand Rapids, Mich.: Inter-Tribal Council, 1986.

Empire (Mich.) Heritage Museum. Booklet, "Some Other Day."

Grand Traverse Convention and Visitors Bureau. Traverse City, Mich. Various written material about fishing and boating.

Leelanau Historical Writers Group. *A History of Leelanau Township.* Friends ofLeelanau Township Library, 1982.

Leelanau Theme Song. Mrs. A. J. Oberham (guest at Fountain Point Resort).

Littell, Edmund H. *One Hundred Years in Leelanau.* Leelanau, Mich.: The PrintShop, 1965. Sponsored by Leelanau County Prospectors Club.

Michigan Department of Natural Resources. Lansing. Various pamphlets about fishing and boating.

References

National Park Service, Department of the Interior. Washington, D.C. NationalLakeshore Brochures.
Quackenbush, Laura. "A Cherry Jubilee." Leemuse, July 1991.
Robbins, Chandler S., Bertel Brunn, and Herbert S. Zim. Birds of North America: *A Guide to Field Identification.* New York: Golden Press, 1983.
Traverse City Record-Eagle. July 19, 1982, and July 18, 1986.
Weeks, George. *Sleeping Bear: Yesterday and Today.* West Bloomfield, Mich.:A&M Publishing Company, 1991.

SEASONS OF THE LEELANAU

Leelinau, Leelinau,
daughter of Indian lore,
are you among the wildflowers
or do you dance along the shore?

A legend you have become,
tall, beautiful, and proud.
Graceful as you're encompassed
by the lake all around.

Manitou, manitou,
each may have their own
to seek from your shore
emerald gems to behold.

Centuries have passed you
as long ago you were.
It is in mens hearts
you are alive, made sure.

Legends people come for,

your beauty to behold.
In that way you are real,
your story ever retold.

Dear maiden, you are resting,
awaiting a paradise so real.
Where legends are the past
and time may forever feel.

And so it goes, Leelanau,
Will man take care of you?
Will they appreciate your beauty
nature so abundantly imbued?

Leelanau, Leelanau
daughter of Indian Lore
You *are* among the wildflowers'
that-dance along the shore.

–Sandra Serra Bradshaw